HIDDEN HISTORY *of*
★ KENTUCKY ★
POLITICAL SCANDALS

ROBERT SCHRAGE AND JOHN SCHAAF

THE
History
PRESS

Published by The History Press
Charleston, SC
www.historypress.com

Front cover, top, left to right: Legislative Research Commission; Library of Congress; Public domain; Library of Congress; Public domain; *bottom*: public domain.
Back cover: Public domain; *inset*: Library of Congress.

First published 2020

Manufactured in the United States

ISBN 9781467145824

Library of Congress Control Number: 2020938481

Notice: The information in this book is true and complete to the best of our knowledge. It is offered without guarantee on the part of the authors or The History Press. The authors and The History Press disclaim all liability in connection with the use of this book.

To all the public servants who work honestly and ethically for the good of the citizens in their communities. Thank you for your commitment to the people.

To Carolyn, Sam, Kevin and Logan.

Contents

CONTENTS

Acknowledgements

The authors wish to thank Kevin T. Kelly, the staff of the Kenton County Library, Ann Schrage, Carolyn Dennis, Trey Grayson, Gene Burch, Bruce Smith, Al Cross, Tom Loftus and Kentucky Legislative Research Commission staff members John McKee, Rob Weber and Steve Gatewood.

INTRODUCTION

Since Kentucky became a state in 1792, generations of its citizens have worked honorably in public service at the state and local government levels. Those public servants and their work are often unappreciated when they should be honored and valued. However, as long as humans are in charge of government, business or any other endeavor, there will be scandals when ethics are set aside in the quest for more wealth, more power or both.

At various points in the state's history, Kentucky's politics and government have been rocked by scandal, and each scandal helped define the era in which it happened. Those scandals produced colorful characters, stories and, in several cases, legal reforms to rebuild public trust and prevent future scandals. Many aspects of Kentucky's experiences are marked by some element of trickery or corruption. Indeed, the state's capital city of Frankfort was founded by General James Wilkinson, whom historian Frederick Jackson Turner called "the most consummate artist in treason that the nation ever possessed."[1] So, there were episodes of corruption and double-dealing before and after statehood, during the post–Civil War years and all the way to the present day with scandals in politics and governing.

Some of the most fascinating stories include State Treasurer "Honest Dick" Tate disappearing forever with bags full of public money, the assassination of Governor William Goebel, Kentucky's political bosses and, more recently, the BOPTROT scandal. Kentucky's motto is "United We Stand, Divided We Fall"; a better motto might be what Pulitzer Prize–winning journalist John Ed Pearce titled his 1987 book: *Divide and Dissent.*

Why does Kentucky have such a history of public scandal? Pearce says, "The ferocity with which Kentuckians play politics and the corruption that so often marks the average courthouse—the vote buying, the patronage, the selling of public services for political loyalty—have their roots in poverty."[2] In addition to its history of economic woes, Kentucky's government power is widely dispersed, with billions of dollars administered by thousands of public officials, all of it flowing to public agencies and private businesses and individuals.

Kentucky has a lot of people working in state and local public service—over thirty-one thousand employees and elected officials in state government and many thousands more who are elected or employed to run the state's 120 counties, the independent entities that Professor Robert Ireland called "Little Kingdoms." Additionally, there are 419 cities, 172 school districts and almost 1,300 special districts that govern everything from airports to water service to tourism and most of which have the power to collect taxes and fees.

With that many people, organizations and sometimes blurry lines of authority, it is amazing there are not more stories of wrongdoing and illegal activity in Kentucky's history. That's a testament to the hundreds of thousands of citizens who've honorably served the commonwealth and its local governments as public employees and elected officials.

The purpose of this book is to look at the unusual and often outrageous episodes: those moments when the darker side of human nature—greed, dishonesty, thirst for power and fraud—infected Kentucky's public life. It would be unfair and inaccurate to conclude that scandals define Kentucky or that Kentucky's scandals are worse or more prevalent than those in other states. Following BOPTROT and other late twentieth-century state and local scandals, Kentucky adopted significant reforms that put the state at the leading edge of anti-corruption laws.

Kentucky has always been a state divided, despite its famous motto. Differences of poverty, geography, tradition, economics and customs all play a role in how the state and its many localities are governed. Those differences also influence the priorities, leadership and, most important, the behavior of the various public officials.

There will always be failures leading to dishonesty and outright corruption in government, business, religion or any institution. The challenge for all of us is to ensure that the institutions are positioned to prevent corruption—or, if it does arise, to address it effectively to maintain or regain the trust of the taxpayers, customers, parishioners and general public.

The authors of this book hope a review of past failings and a discussion of effective reforms will help lead to an awareness of how good we can be. As Shakespeare wrote in *All's Well That Ends Well*, "No legacy is so rich as honesty." Perhaps a new tradition has started!

THE EARLY YEARS

Statehood and the Start of a Kentucky Tradition

P eople often think of political scandal as a modern-day occurrence, but nothing could be further from the truth. The prevalence of scandals began in earnest in the mid- to late 1800s, across the country and certainly in Kentucky. In the early days of the commonwealth, government didn't have a lot of money, so theft of public funds was not a significant source of scandal. It was not until state government had revenue to steal that financial scandals took off. Nonetheless, the early years before and after statehood were divisive and, in some ways, scandalous. To fully understand the hidden history of Kentucky political scandals, it is helpful to review those early years and the various occurrences leading to the establishment of traditions that have lasted for more than two centuries.

STATEHOOD

Kentucky was born out of the Commonwealth of Virginia, a large mass of land stretching east to west approximately 800 miles in the late 1700s. As Patricia Watlington observes in her book *The Partisan Spirit*, Virginia "suffered from a hump on her back, the Allegheny Mountains that lay in ridges from north to south, forming a series of barriers between Virginia and Kentucky proper." The mountains were tall, 250 miles across and populated with Native Americans.[1] Beyond these mountains was the future, where the New

World, including Kentucky, would grow. It took a rugged spirit to settle these beautiful lands, and from those pioneers grew the new commonwealth called Kentucky. However, settlement was difficult and fraught with controversy. The road to becoming a state would be divisive, and it can be argued that the first scandal happened even before statehood.

So, what would create that first scandal? In a few words: land laws and land grants. The first controversy involved whether Virginia even owned Kentucky. The first land companies argued that the king never granted Kentucky to Virginia; however, it was included in the 1609 Charter. The companies claimed that the land was granted to the entire nation and was under the jurisdiction of the Continental Congress. Of course, there was money involved. According to *The Partisan Spirit*, "most of the land companies were operated out of Philadelphia and could profit from the Virginia claim, but a congressional claim would mean they might cash in on their purchases of land from Indians. They evidently hoped to receive congressional land grants and then sell the land in small parcels at high prices."[2]

The Virginia land laws of 1779 resolved the issue by giving land to settlers under their claims. Virginia then encouraged individuals, especially military veterans, to take up claims. First, a warrant was necessary, but that was of no use if it did not include an attachment of specific land. Thus, settlers went off to Kentucky to find prime land. From 1777 to 1779, settlers came to Kentucky in large numbers, and many were not of upstanding character. One group was land surveyors hoping to make good money after braving the harsh trip from Virginia, Pennsylvania or North Carolina. It stands to reason that Kentucky's earliest scandal involved land surveyors.

Patricia Watlington called Thomas Hamilton "the oldest and best established of the surveyors." He was fifty-two when he became surveyor of Fayette County in 1781, eleven years before statehood. He was a tall, slender man who had previously served in the Virginia legislature. He designated his nephew Humphrey Marshall as his deputy surveyor and began a political scandal. Humphrey was enthusiastic and wanted to tap into the riches of land speculation. He seemed "capable of any deceit that would increase his wealth."[3]

As a public surveyor with a streak of dishonesty, Marshall was entangled in several schemes. One involved charging a double fee—when people could not pay it after twelve months, they lost their plats. As the first to know, Marshall would swoop in and put the plats in his name.

Marshall was involved in other complicated schemes to grab land. Surveyors often took advantage of poor individuals who knew no better, and almost all surveyors obtained great quantities of land. Marshall acquired 97,316 acres, and John May, another surveyor, amassed 831,294 acres of Kentucky.[4] Virginia established Kentucky counties; perhaps Marshall was the first of many corrupt county officials in Kentucky history.

The development of Kentucky politics can be seen in many ways through its constitution. Kentucky statehood was all but assured by the Virginia Compact of 1789, but it took three more years and ten conventions (between 1784 and 1792) to achieve independence. According to Mary K. Bonsteel Tachau in *The Kentucky Encyclopedia*, "The principal obstacles to separation involved Virginia land grants and the shared responsibilities for Virginia's debt from the Revolutionary War." The terms of the compact were revised to the satisfaction of Kentucky, and it was admitted as the fifteenth state in 1792.

Kentucky's first Constitutional Convention was held in 1792. Modeled on Virginia's charter, that first constitution called for a lower house of legislators to serve one-year terms and appoint the state senate and governor for four-year terms. It also established a court of appeals, the state's highest court. This constitution was not submitted to the voters but established a process for a new convention in a few years.

Controversies in the various branches of government resulted in a new convention in 1799. Two major controversies at the time included a decision by the Kentucky Court of Appeals in 1794, setting off Kentucky's first major political fight. The decision held that the Virginia Land Commission exceeded its authority when it decided the rights of numerous land disputes in Kentucky during the years of 1779 and 1780. This undermined the land titles of thousands of Kentuckians and resulted in the legislature attempting to remove two justices who had voted in favor of the decision. The attempt failed, but the legislature later took the jurisdiction of the court of appeals over land cases.[5]

The second controversy involved the disputed governor's race of 1796. James Garrard was a candidate, along with Ben Logan and Thomas Todd. Logan was the favorite because he was a military hero; Todd had served as secretary of all ten statehood conventions. The Kentucky Electoral College did not give any of four candidates for governor a majority vote, and instead of giving the candidate with the most votes (Logan) the office, "conducted a second ballot between the top two highest vote getters."[6] The second-place candidate was Garrard. On the second ballot, Garrard was victorious and declared the next governor. Logan protested but eventually gave up the effort. Garrard succeeded Isaac Shelby, the first governor of Kentucky.

Left: Kentucky's first governor, Isaac Shelby. *Library of Congress*.

Right: Kentucky governor James Garrard. *Public domain*.

While none of this was illegal, it was a huge political controversy and one of the first episodes in a long history of election-related strife and division in Kentucky. Garrard would go on to succeed himself and be the last governor to do so until a constitutional amendment allowed succession in 1992. Paul Patton was reelected in 1999 and was the first governor since Garrard to win consecutive terms.

THE START OF A KENTUCKY TRADITION

A few decades after statehood, Kentucky experienced what Professor Frank F. Mathias declared "the turbulent years of Kentucky politics: 1820–1850." This period certainly built upon the first years of the commonwealth's divisiveness to create an era when political parties and sectionalism started. These issues still divide the state, as do economics, poverty and tradition.

The 1799 Constitutional Convention made some changes to Kentucky's first constitution. The governor was able to keep his important patronage power, with the authority to appoint the judiciary, but slavery remained protected, as it had been in 1792. One of the most important differences of opinion concerned the requirement that only property owners were entitled to vote. This argument had gone on since the beginning of statehood. As Mathias says, "Those with no property wanted no property qualification for voting and wanted a bill of rights and suffrage for 'free white males.'"[7] He points out that there was much suspicion between landowners and those without land.

Restrictions on suffrage of free white males were not part of the 1799 constitution, so property owners continued to want some checks on democracy, including indirect election of the governor and state senators and control of the judiciary. However, this second constitutional convention angered property owners by changing the anti-democracy 1792 constitution to provide for direct election of the governor and state senators, abolishing the Electoral College and prohibiting the governor from succeeding himself. More than anything else, this division led to the formation of political parties.

While the party movement was gaining traction across the nation, Kentucky was divided along property and then party lines. Kentucky would become known for citizens showing often blind loyalty to political parties and the leaders who ran them. This tradition started in the early 1800s and lasted until late in the twentieth century. As the parties matured, however, issues did become more important, and voters took sides between the likes of Henry Clay, a Whig, or Andrew Jackson, a Democrat. National politics had significant influence on Kentucky.

The governors during this time were heavily involved in patronage, and loyalty to party was vital for appointments. The governor was usually the face of the party, and it was important to his future success, including national aspirations, to have loyal appointments throughout the state. Extreme political patronage like this would be an issue in state and federal politics until the reform movement forty to sixty years down the road.

Kentucky did not recognize the legal existence of political parties until 1842.[8] However, they in fact had existed since the 1820s, evolving over the years following the last constitutional convention. Just like today, one of the early problems for legislators in Kentucky was setting up voting areas and other aspects of election administration. With the advent of parties, elected officials often considered the impact of changes in legislation on their party. Any advantages the laws gave their opponents were troublesome. Mathias is correct when he says that the "evolution of election administration was slow and tortuous."[9] As a result, calls for honest elections administered in a nonpartisan manner were nonexistent. It would take almost a century to clean up the electoral mess, and dissent and fraud now had a system in place to flourish.

Thomas N. Lindsey, a representative and a delegate to the 1849 constitutional convention, said in a letter to Orlando Brown, "Kentucky elections are annual 'scenes' that last for three days." Elections originally were held in the county seat but dispersed as population scattered, leading to the creation of many more polling places. Mathias said that voice voting was held and that one's party affiliation and political leanings were known to all. Election Day drinking and fighting were commonplace, and "lengthy elections offered the opportunities and time for party workers to organize themselves toward the perpetration of frauds." For example, in the 1836 presidential election, Gallatin County had 918 voters registered but a total of 1,008 voted, resulting in 109.8 percent turnout. In 1832, at least five counties exceeded 100 percent of their possible vote. Oldham County went so far as to have 163.1 percent of its possible votes.[10] For the most part, the county sheriff was responsible for state and local elections. If voter fraud existed, the sheriff usually knew about it—and sometimes was in the middle of it.

In 1833, a major case of election fraud happened in a congressional district covering several rural counties. In the election, Thomas P. Moore and Robert P. Letcher contested their race, which was held in the Fifth Congressional District. The controversy happened when five county sheriffs met to compare votes. Each was a strong partisan, loyal to their candidate and party. Moore was a Democrat and Letcher a Whig. Four of the counties' totals were in doubt. The fifth county went for Letcher, but the sheriff walked out, and the remaining counties certified the election for Moore, however, the U.S. House refused to seat either candidate and ordered a new election, which Letcher won by 258 votes. This was a good example of the need for nonpartisan election administration.

In the first half of the nineteenth century, Kentucky's political parties were defined by economic and cultural events. In their second edition of *A New History of Kentucky*, Klotter and Friend say that "economic, religious, personal and societal" events affected every Kentuckian, but "there was little agreement on how to improve society....One side felt if left alone, in time[people] would do what was right. Others believed that people could be trusted only when their character had been transformed, whether by conversion, reform movements, or even government." This was the fundamental difference between the Whigs and the Democrats in Kentucky.

Such deeply held personal but opposite beliefs influenced the type of behavior fundamental to fraud.

With all this said, Kentucky's geography may have affected its politics more than any other factor. Some, including Mathias, believe the natural geographic division was ignored when Kentucky was laid out and its borders established. He says, "Sectionalism thrives best when arbitrary borders frustrate nature's design, and Kentucky's subsequent history would seem to approve this statement."

James Wilkinson

James Wilkinson is one of the most controversial figures in the early years of Kentucky and the nation. Wilkinson was born in Maryland in 1757. His record is both amazing and controversial. He served in the Continental army during the American Revolutionary War, first in Thompson's Pennsylvania Battalion from 1775 to 1776. He was commissioned a captain in 1775 and served as an aide to Nathanael Greene during the siege of Boston. Following the British withdrawal from Boston, Wilkinson went to New York, left Greene's staff and was given command of an infantry company. According to his Wikipedia entry, he "was sent to Canada as part of reinforcements for Benedict Arnold's army besieging Quebec. He arrived just in time to witness the arrival of 8,000 British reinforcements under General John Burgoyne." This led to the collapse of the American forces and caused their retreat.

Wilkinson became an aide to Arnold and soon thereafter to General Horatio Gates. Gates gave Wilkinson the honor of going before Congress to deliver news of victory at Saratoga. According to Steve Preston, writing in NKyTribune, "Not only did Wilkinson keep Congress waiting while attending to personal matters, when he finally did appear, he inflated his own role in the victory." As a result, he was given the brevet rank of brigadier general, and he was just twenty years old. His long history of deceit had begun. He was also appointed to the U.S. Board of War and Ordnance. Again, according to his Wikipedia entry, "The promotion over more senior colonels caused uproar among Continental officers, especially because Wilkinson's gossiping seemed to indicate he was a participant in the Conway Cabal conspiracy to replace George Washington with Horatio Gates as Commander-in-Chief of the Continental Army." As a result, he was forced to resign in March 1778.

Following some service in the Pennsylvania militia and in that state's assembly, he moved to Kentucky in 1784, eight years before statehood. Based on his Revolutionary War record, it may appear that Wilkinson was a hero and a valiant public servant, but the problem is that Wilkinson was a traitor! His actions while in Kentucky created the state's first major scandal with national implications.

There were two strong sides on the issue of Kentucky's proposed secession from Virginia: remain a part of Virginia or become a separate state. However, there was a third, more secretive proposal led by Wilkinson, and that was for Kentucky to secede from the Union and become part of the Spanish empire. In 1787, Wilkinson traveled from Kentucky to New Orleans to meet with the governor of Louisiana, Esteban Rodriguez Miro. In an amazing feat of treachery and arrogance, Wilkinson, according to Klotter and Friend in *A New History of Kentucky*, "convinced the Louisiana Governor that he could deliver Kentucky into the Spanish orbit and, by directing immigration into the Mississippi River Valley, prevent an American invasion of Spanish territory. In return, he wanted a trade monopoly, a royal pension, and a rank and position in the Spanish military." Wilkinson would thus control the only means by which individuals could send goods from Kentucky to Louisiana.

At home, Wilkinson would advocate for Kentucky's separation from both Virginia and the United States.

Rumors continued about his dealings with the Spanish government, but no proof existed, and he was not charged. According to Preston, Wilkinson signed a document pledging his loyalty to the Spanish Crown. Later, Wilkinson would receive a $7,000 pension from Miro.

James Wilkinson. *Library of Congress.*

Kentucky joined the Union on June 1, 1792. Wilkinson had begun his second military career. He became active in leading Kentucky volunteers to fight Indians. His activities as a traitor were put on hold. Wilkinson wanted to get back into the military and did so when he was appointed a lieutenant colonel. Later, President Washington was looking for a new general and, after consideration, rejected Wilkinson for Anthony Wayne. Wilkinson was made brigadier general.

As Preston says, "A Spanish spy now held the number two post in the United States Army."

During this time, Wilkinson would pass on secrets to the Spanish, including strategy and troop movements. With the death of Wayne, Wilkinson became commander of the United States Army. He was still being paid to spy by the Spanish government. According to author Thomas Jewett in his article "James Wilkinson: America's Greatest Scoundrel," published by *Archiving Early America*, "The citizens of Detroit protested his greed so much that Wilkinson was transferred and named Commander of the Army's Southern Department. After arriving in the South, Wilkinson wheeled and dealed in land speculation and Army contracts." While in New Orleans to take possession of the Louisiana Purchase, Wilkinson purportedly received a $12,000 bribe from the Spanish. He advised the Spanish on holding off American expansion in exchange for restoration of his pension. According to Wikipedia, he tipped off the Spanish to the purpose of the expedition of Lewis and Clark and "provided advice to the Marquess of Casa Calvo to aid in the negotiations over the Texas-Louisiana border."

Wilkinson was one of Aaron Burr's chief cohorts in the Burr conspiracy—the plan to create an independent country in the middle of North America, including the southwest United States and Mexico. Burr persuaded President Thomas Jefferson to appoint Wilkinson as governor of the Louisiana Territory, but Wilkinson would later send a letter to Jefferson stating that he believed this was evidence of Burr's treason. He was afraid his own involvement in the conspiracy might be revealed. For the wrong reasons, Wilkinson helped break up the conspiracy.

Wilkinson would later go on to serve ineffectively in the War of 1812, and he went to Mexico following the end of his military career. According to Jewett, "Using the guise as an agent of the American Bible Society, he traveled to Mexico and bilked the government out of a Texas land grant."

The Spanish called Wilkinson by the code name "Agent 13," and his involvement with spying for the Spanish was suspected, but there was no proof. Many people had no idea about his spying activities. However, in 1854, Louisiana historian Charles Gayarre published Wilkinson's correspondence with Miro. Others followed with more proof of his activities. In later years, Theodore Roosevelt would say about Wilkinson, "In all our history, there is no more despicable character." Thomas Jewett says Wilkinson was "a man who lied and cheated throughout his entire life." He was perhaps Kentucky's first major scandalous figure, and he died in Mexico in 1825.

GOVERNOR JOSEPH DESHA

Joseph Desha served as Kentucky's ninth governor from 1824 to 1828. He was born in Pennsylvania in 1768 and eventually settled in Mason County, Kentucky. He was a farmer who served in both the Indian War of 1794 and in the War of 1812. Desha was a member of the Kentucky House of Representatives and the state senate and, from 1807 to 1819, a member of the U.S. House of Representatives. Elected governor in 1824, he served four turbulent years. It is difficult to rank more than fifty governors who've presided over two centuries of statehood; however, the case can be made that Desha is the worst.

There were several controversies during Desha's term, but one in particular was downright scandalous, and it involved his family. The trial for the murder of Francis Baker, held in 1825, was a high-profile case because the accused was Isaac Desha, the son of the governor of Kentucky. The murder took place the year Joseph was elected governor. While visiting from Mississippi, Baker was robbed and murdered. According to author Berry Craig, Baker's body was "bloody, beaten, stabbed and stripped." He was reportedly killed with a leaded horsewhip and a knife.

Prior to its start in 1825, the trial moved to the governor's home county of Harrison. The judge who moved the trial, George "Peg Leg" Shannon, was a friend of the governor. Isaac's attorneys included a friend of the governor and member of the state's highest court. The jury found Desha guilty of murder and robbery and decided on death as the penalty. Judge Shannon decided that the trial evidence was "tainted," set aside the verdict and ordered a new trial.

The judge's decision caused widespread public anger. A new trial was held in 1826. Again, Isaac was found guilty and ordered to meet the hangman. Isaac then tried to kill himself and was soon pardoned by his father. The pardon was issued despite Isaac's guilt being clearly proven in the two trials. Nobody thought he would survive the attempted suicide, but he did, and he was a free man. According to Craig, "After the trial, a lot of people got the idea that in Kentucky if you were well connected, you could get away with murder—literally."

The decision to pardon was extremely controversial, and public criticism rained down on the governor. When his term ended, Desha retired to his farm near Cynthiana and died in 1842. Baker's murder and Desha's interference in the legal process and pardoning his son after two convictions appears to be Kentucky's first major scandal involving a family member of a top political figure. Isaac left the state and later confessed to committing another murder, this time in Texas.

Congressman Kills Colleague in Duel

William Graves was born in New Castle, Kentucky, in 1805. He decided early in life to pursue a legal career. He was admitted to the bar in Kentucky, was elected to the Kentucky House of Representatives and served in 1834 before being elected to the Twenty-Fourth Congress and serving three terms, from 1835 to 1841.

Jonathan Cilley was born in 1802 in Nottingham, New Hampshire. Interestingly, Cilley graduated from Bowdoin College in Maine with Nathaniel Hawthorne and Henry Wadsworth Longfellow. He became good friends with future president Franklin Pierce, who also graduated from Bowdoin. Cilley decided to stay in Maine, where he was admitted to the bar in 1828 and became a member of the Maine House of Representatives in 1831. He served as Speaker of the Maine House of Representatives in 1835 and 1836, and was elected to the U.S. House of Representatives in 1836.

It was in Congress where Graves and Cilley met, eventually resulting in a deadly duel. By the end of the Twenty-Fifth session of Congress, partisanship was high. Graves, originally elected as an anti-Jacksonian, was elected as a Whig in later elections. Cilley was a Democrat. A central figure to the eventual duel between Graves and Cilley was New York newspaper editor James Watson Webb, a biased journalist who was a loyal Whig. Cilley called Webb corrupt and asserted that his reporting of Congress was biased and unfair.[11] Cilley stated on the House floor what many of his party believed— that Webb changed from opposing to supporting the re-chartering of the Second Bank of the United States because he had received loans from the bank totaling $52,000.[12] Webb was greatly insulted by the allegations and convinced Graves to act on his behalf in extending his challenge to a duel against Cilley. A letter of challenge from Webb was to be delivered to Cilley by Graves, but Cilley refused to accept the letter, which Graves took as an insult. Thus, Graves challenged Cilley, who then accepted.

Dueling was illegal in the District of Columbia, so the parties agreed to meet at the Bladensburg Dueling Grounds in Maryland, just outside the

Left: Jonathan Cilley. *Library of Congress*. *Right*: William Graves. *Public domain*.

District. The dueling grounds saw approximately fifty duels over a sixty-year period beginning in 1808. The most famous duel held at Bladensburg, according to Wikipedia, happened in June 1836, when "22-year-old Daniel Key, the son of Francis Scott Key, was killed in a senseless duel with a fellow Naval Academy midshipman John Sherbourne over a question regarding steamboat speed."

The Graves-Cilley duel happened on February 24, 1838. Cilley had the choice of weapons and selected rifles. Graves was an excellent marksman with pistols, thus the selection of rifles by Cilley. The distance was set off at eighty yards but reportedly was actually ninety-four yards. The first shots missed, and the distance was shortened. Again, the shots missed. On the third attempt, Graves hit Cilley in the femoral artery, fatally wounding him. He died within a few minutes.

In 1839, Congress passed an act prohibiting issuing a challenge or accepting a duel in the boundaries of the District of Columbia, no matter where the duel would be fought. Congressman Graves did not seek reelection in 1840 and, after serving again in the Kentucky House of Representatives, died in Louisville in 1848. He is buried at his former residence in Henry County. Cilley didn't finish his one term in Congress and is buried in Maine. Webb would go on to serve as minister to Brazil for eight years. He died in 1884.

CONCLUSION

The turbulent period of the early to mid-1800s established traditions related to election fraud and political scandal that lasted for generations. The period was rarely free of double-dealing and fraudulent election campaigns. The advent of political parties meant that issues were not as important as personalities and party loyalty. The lack of efficient, nonpartisan election administration perpetuated fraud. Voters and politicians rationalized that cheating was for a greater good. The remainder of this book will highlight the results that evolved from this belief.

The Century's Last Fifty Years

1850–1900

The second half of the 1800s accounted for some of the most divisive years in Kentucky history. They were marked by the unsettling times following the end of the Civil War, violence and new political scandals. The end of the Civil War brought about political and social change to which Kentuckians struggled to adapt. Kentucky was at first a neutral state and later had strong Union support during the war. Violence related to elections, newly freed slaves getting the right to vote and general lawlessness dominated the years after the war.

During this era, there were several major political scandals, including the Thomas Page Affair, the James W. "Honest Dick" Tate abscension, the shooting of a former congressman and events surrounding the assassination of Governor William Goebel.

The Thomas Page Affair

Thomas Page was the first elected public auditor for the State of Kentucky and served from 1851 to 1859. Prior to that, Page had been appointed auditor in 1839 by Governor James Clark. The position was created by the legislature as a temporary two-year position, but it was made permanent in 1843, and Page was re-appointed each two-year period until the new constitution eliminated the position in 1850. The new constitution made the position elective instead of appointed and made it a constitutional office.

In 1851, Page ran for the office and won. He was the last appointed auditor in the state's history and the first to be elected.

Page was born in New York in 1800 and came to Kentucky in 1817. He was extremely ambitious and a hard worker. It did not take him long to become successful, and he began "taking advantage of investment and business opportunities among the Frankfort elite."[1] He became involved in civic affairs, including the Masons and in private enterprises. He started accumulating land, first in Louisville and then in Oldham County. His wealth was also established through two marriages, including his first to Sophia Woolfolk, who died in 1828. The same year, he married Jane Julian, and they eventually had eleven children. In the 1830s, his business activities and investments continued to grow, and in 1833, he had an assessed worth of $13,400, which included four slaves. By the end of the decade, he had an assessed worth of $27,095, including ten slaves, 980 acres and horses and cattle.[2] In February 1839, Governor Clark appointed him auditor.

In this position, he was able to establish political contacts around the state, including with local sheriffs and justices of the peace. He was responsible for collecting and supervising the disbursement of "ordinary public revenue."

He was a loyal Whig, and after serving as the appointed auditor, his party nominated him to run for the first elected auditor position in 1851. He was unopposed, so he was elected. The auditor was perhaps, second to the governor, the most powerful position in the state. By 1855, Page joined the anti-Catholic, anti-immigration Know-Nothing Party and won reelection. As mentioned, he served until 1859, when he lost his bid for a third term. His successor was Grant Green, who beat Page in a narrow election.

Unbeknownst to anyone (maybe somebody knew and didn't disclose it), as auditor, Page embezzled $88,927 by having local officials deposit their revenue with him as opposed to in the state treasury, as required by law. During his time in office, his wealth grew tremendously. According to Glen Tau and Dennis Fielding, in their article "Politics and Corruption in Antebellum Kentucky," "The assessed value of Page's personal estate increased from $27,095 in 1839 to $40,450 in 1852. Taxable property for 1859, 1860 and 1861 was assessed at $70,000, $82,000, and $64,000 respectively." This was not his total wealth, as it excludes accounts and assets in other states. His account, according to Tau and Fielding, "at Farmers Bank of Kentucky was reported as $120,000 on January 1, 1858 and $110,000 on January 1, 1860."

Tau and Fielding describe his duties well: "The Auditor's primary source of effective political power was his authority to supervise the collection of the general revenue from every local official in the state and gathering of taxes and fees from every turnpike, road, and railroad company, bank and savings institution, insurance company, and corporation. The State Treasurer could only receive funds upon written authority from the Auditor and could only disburse money upon the Auditor's warrant. The Auditor held more effective control over the state's money than either the Governor or the General Assembly."

Grant Green became auditor on January 2, 1860. He kept Page on as a contractor for approximately two years, working on the "daily journal, general ledger and individual account ledgers, even taking some of the ledgers home." Green had to work to get some of the ledgers back after Page left the auditor's office. Then, in September 1862, impropriety was found. It was also during this time that it appeared Page was having financial difficulties. Perhaps these difficulties started earlier and were the reason for the embezzlement. Page would eventually declare himself broke but would try and pay some money back in restitution. There was no way Page was going to be able to pay the total of the embezzled money back, so Green informed Governor James Robinson.

It is worth noting that the crimes of which Page was obviously guilty were not criminal under Kentucky law at the time. The Code of Practice in Criminal Cases said, "All public offenses may be prosecuted by indictment except" for public officials. The remedy for collection of the auditor's theft was through a $100,000 bond with surety that Page was required to post. In essence, the auditor and the bondholders were liable. It was a civil, not criminal, matter.

Page was the first Kentucky elected official to be charged with embezzlement.

The state filed lawsuits claiming much wrongdoing by Page, alleging that he didn't "faithfully discharge" the duties of his office. Of course, the bondholders argued many points to assert their lack of liability. Most interesting was the argument that "the breaches would have been prevented had the legislature fulfilled its legal responsibility. At each regular session, the General Assembly was required by law to appoint a joint committee to examine the operation of the Auditor's office and to make a report to both houses. Such a committee had never been appointed."[3]

Grave of Thomas Page. *Photo by Robert Schrage.*

Eventually, Page would agree to pay $13,000 in the first case and $75,000 in the second. With fees and court costs, it totaled $90,082.20.[4] On November 12, 1867, Page's trustee paid the state $45,041.10 from his estate, so the state collected about half the embezzled amount.

Page, along with his second wife, lived his remaining years in poverty in Frankfort, where he died on April 17, 1877. He is buried in Frankfort Cemetery. His wife, Jane, died in 1889. Grant Green died in 1898 at the age of seventy-two and is buried not far from Thomas Page.

Union General Stephen Burbridge: The "Butcher of Kentucky"?

Kentucky's deadliest Civil War battles were fought in 1862 and early 1863, but during the last two years of the war, there were numerous attacks on people and property throughout the state, and most were perpetrated by groups of Confederate soldiers, ex-Confederates or Southern-sympathizing marauders.

Throughout the war, Kentucky's state government stayed loyal to the United States and did not secede from the Union. However, President Abraham Lincoln and his military commanders believed they had to develop an effective response to Confederate guerrilla attacks and suppress many of the political activities of Kentucky civilians who supported the Southern cause.

In February 1864, General Ulysses Grant appointed General Stephen Burbridge to temporarily command most of Kentucky except for the far western region. A few months later, Burbridge's command was made "permanent." However, by February 1865, his policies and tactics had alienated Kentuckians, and he was replaced for the final months of the war.

Burbridge was a native Kentuckian, born in Scott County in 1831. When the Civil War began, he organized the Twenty-Sixth Kentucky Union Infantry and served as its colonel. He fought at the Battle of Shiloh and in the Vicksburg Campaign and was a high-ranking officer under General William Tecumseh Sherman, who would later become Burbridge's trusted adviser.[5]

During the first half of 1864, Burbridge's command of Kentucky had the support of Governor Thomas Bramlette, who was a "Union Democrat" and a friend of Burbridge's. However, the relationship soured as Burbridge implemented the orders he was getting from Washington, D.C.

On July 5, 1864, President Lincoln issued a proclamation declaring martial law in Kentucky and suspending the writ of habeas corpus, allowing the military to arrest people suspected of disloyalty and hold them indefinitely. Lincoln's proclamation was primarily aimed at Kentuckians who "joined the forces of the insurgents," but it was also directed at Kentuckians who the president said were "inciting rebel forces to renew the civil war within the state," "embarrassing the United States armies operating in Virginia and Georgia, and even endangering their safety."[6]

Less than two weeks later, on July 16, Burbridge issued his infamous Order No. 59. He no doubt thought he was taking steps necessary to implement the president's proclamation, but the order and his subsequent actions labeled him the "Butcher of Kentucky."

In the order, Burbridge states that "all guerrillas, armed prowlers by whatever name they may be known, and rebel sympathizers, are hereby admonished that in future stern retaliatory measures will be adopted and strictly enforced whenever the lives or property of peaceful citizens are jeopardized by the lawless acts of such men.…

"Wherever an unarmed Union citizen is murdered, four guerrillas will be selected from the prisoners in the hands of the military authorities and publicly shot to death in the most convenient place near the scene of outrage."[7]

Starting on July 19 with the execution of two prisoners in Louisville, the retaliatory killings went on for the next several months all over the state—two shot in Russellville on July 29, four in Eminence on August 12, five on August 15 in Grant and Nelson Counties, four in Meade County in early September and on and on.

Usually, the executions were carried out on two, three or four prisoners at a time, in Frankfort, Maysville, Pleasureville, Bloomfield, Midway, Jeffersontown and elsewhere. Then, on November 19, fourteen men were executed in Hart County, and the executions continued until the last one was carried out in Christian County on January 10, 1865. It's estimated that about two hundred citizens and Confederate prisoners died in this manner.[8]

Burbridge's ordered killings were ineffective in stemming the tide of guerrilla raids that continued to spread murder and mayhem throughout Kentucky. He was also heavy handed and ineffective in his attempts to suppress political dissent, which he saw as threatening to the Union cause.

Burbridge interfered with two Kentucky elections in 1864. The first interference was in August, three days before a state election, when he ordered the name of an incumbent judge stricken from the ballot on the grounds that the judge was a Confederate sympathizer. Then, in the weeks

General Stephen Burbridge. *Public domain.*

preceding the November presidential election, Burbridge characterized large numbers of Kentuckians as disloyal to the Union, ordered their arrests (including the lieutenant governor, the state's chief justice and the editors of the *Louisville Journal* and the *Owensboro Monitor*) and banished them from the state.

On the day of the election, Burbridge deployed Federal troops to polling places in a move that probably felt to many Kentucky voters like intimidation and an effort to suppress support for George McClellan, Lincoln's opponent. In spite of Burbridge's efforts, McClellan easily carried Kentucky, although Lincoln won the national election by a wide margin. McClellan's win in Kentucky was an indication of the unpopularity of Lincoln's policies as carried out in the state by Burbridge.

In the months in which he was in command of Kentucky, Burbridge used a very heavy hand to implement many wartime policies promulgated by the United States. It's reasonable to believe that his overly forceful approach alienated many Kentuckians from their loyalty to the federal government. After the war ended, Kentucky voters elected Confederate sympathizers and ex-soldiers to run the state government for the next three decades.

Because he was so widely hated in his native state, Burbridge moved to Brooklyn, New York, after the war and died there in December 1894. He is buried in Arlington National Cemetery, across the Potomac River from Washington, D.C.

The Aftermath of the Civil War

Reconstruction of the South was the major federal initiative the United States pursued following the war. It was intended to change the racist system that had existed in the states of the Confederacy, and it had a somewhat lesser impact in Kentucky than in states in the Deep South. However, Kentucky's response to Reconstruction was similar to that of other southern states. It had conservative Democrats opposing the new set of norms and policies advocated by the federal government and "radical" Republicans who supported change. Klotter and Friend wrote, "Kentucky went through a period not of Reconstruction but of Readjustment."

Following the Civil War, Kentucky politics was deeply divided and saw vicious infighting between and inside of the political parties, especially as leaders fought emancipation and civil rights for freed slaves. Citizens, party loyalists and elected officials pushed back against changes that were inevitable following the war. This was particularly true of federal efforts at passing the three Reconstruction amendments to the Constitution.

The Thirteenth, Fourteenth and Fifteenth Amendments were all proposed in response to issues related to former slaves. The Thirteenth Amendment abolished slavery. The Fourteenth addressed citizens' rights and equal protection, and the Fifteenth Amendment gave African Americans the right to vote. Tapp and Klotter point out that slavery in

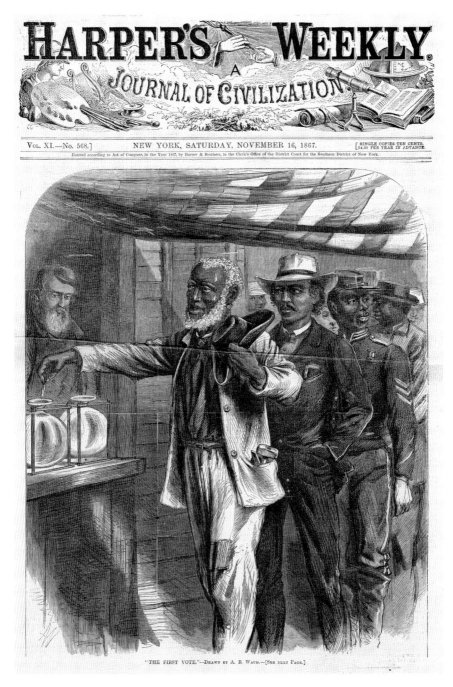

The First Vote, by Alfred Waud. *Library of Congress.*

again in 1882. He was a farmer and had served as a state senator. In 1881, he was admitted to the bar.

Charles E. Kincaid, a *Louisville Times* Washington correspondent, reported in 1888 that Congressman Taulbee was found in a "compromising way" with a young woman in the U.S. Patent Office. According to Berry Craig in *True Tales of Old-Time Kentucky Politics*, Kincaid claimed the woman was "a little daisy, bright as a sunbeam and saucy as a bowl of jelly; petite of figure but plump as a partridge." The scandal marked the end of Taulbee's political career. Over the next couple of years, Taulbee and Kincaid would run into each other in the Capitol. Taulbee had become a lobbyist and would insult Kincaid when they crossed paths. In a story on National Public Radio, historian James Klotter said, "As they passed each other, the Congressman would pull on the reporter's nose or ear."

"On February 28, 1890, Taulbee came across Kincaid at the Capitol and threatened the journalist. According to a Capitol doorkeeper who witnessed the threat, ex-Congressman Taulbee grabbed Kincaid by his coat collar and said 'Kincaid, come out into the corridor with me.' Kincaid responded to Taulbee's actions by saying that he was 'in no condition for a physical contest' and that he was unarmed. Mutual friends separated the two men."[20] According to History.house.gov, "The two traded verbal insults and 'the tall and sinewy' Taulbee allegedly warned the slight reporter—described in a contemporary account as a 'little pint-of-cider fellow' to arm himself." Klotter says it this way: "The strapping Taulbee, about a foot taller than the frail, five-foot, three-inch Kincaid, warned the reporter he had better arm himself."[21]

A couple hours later, Kincaid and Taulbee saw each other again in the U.S. Capitol Building. Kincaid drew a revolver and shot Taulbee in the face, one and a quarter inches from his left eye. Kincaid made no effort to run away and admitted to the shooting. Physicians and a congressman cared for Taulbee and thought he would recover. Kincaid was taken into custody and moved to the police station on New Jersey Avenue. Unfortunately, Taulbee died on March 11, and Kincaid was charged with murder.

The shooting perpetuated the image of Kentucky as a violent state. During the trial, two witnesses claimed they saw the shooting. The trial took place between March 23 and April 8, 1891. Despite the evidence, Kincaid was acquitted. In *A New History of Kentucky*, Klotter and Friend write that the acquittal was "on the grounds that he reacted to threats as a gentleman would."

According to Encyclopedia.com, "During the trial, eight current and former members of Congress, as well as a number of newspapermen, testified about Taulbee's numerous threats against Kincaid. One said that Taulbee frequently remarked that he ought to kill Kincaid because Kincaid had ruined his and his family's reputation. Another indicated that Taulbee threatened to kick Kincaid's head off if the correspondent ever came within ten feet of him. A third quoted Taulbee as saying, 'He [Kincaid] ought to be killed. By God, I'll kill him.' Many of these witnesses warned Kincaid about the threats and this, according to the defense lawyers, contributed to their client's fears for his life."

Following the trial, Kincaid returned to Kentucky and later served on the Kentucky Railroad Commission and as an American diplomat. In 1896, he became a reporter for the *Cincinnati Enquirer*, and he died in 1906 at the age of fifty-one.

To this day, the blood of William Preston Taulbee still stains the marble steps in the U.S. Capitol where he was shot.

THE POLLARD-BRECKINRIDGE SCANDAL

Perhaps in Kentucky history there is no name more well known or significant than that of Breckinridge. As James Klotter says in his well-respected book *The Breckinridges of Kentucky: 1760–1981*, "Statistics support the claim, for in the first half of the sixty-eight years of Kentucky statehood a Breckinridge had served in either state or the national capital." The name is synonymous with public service—not only for a few years, but also throughout the history of Kentucky. There was John Breckinridge (1760–1806), who served in the Virginia legislature, as Kentucky's attorney general and as Speaker of the House. He served under President Thomas Jefferson as attorney general and was a U.S. senator. His son Robert Jefferson Breckinridge (1800–1871) also served in the Kentucky General Assembly and was, according to Klotter, a "Whig antislavery leader in the State." He was called the father of Kentucky's public education system.[22]

William Campbell Preston Breckinridge was the son of Robert Jefferson and was born on August 28, 1837. He graduated from Centre College and after studying to be a doctor for a year changed to law. In 1857, he graduated from the University of Louisville with a juris doctorate and went to Lexington to practice. He married his first wife, Lucretia Clay, a granddaughter of Henry Clay, in 1859. She died in 1860, and in 1861, he married Issa Desha.

William Campbell Preston Breckinridge. *Library of Congress.*

Unlike most in his immediate family, William supported the Confederacy in the Civil War and rode with John Hunt Morgan. Later in the war, he was a colonel with the Ninth Kentucky Cavalry. According to Wikipedia, "He also served as a bodyguard to Jefferson Davis during his flight from Richmond." After the war, William returned to Lexington to practice law and from 1866 to 1868 was the editor of the *Lexington Observer and Reporter*.

Following the war, William Breckinridge had a major transformation, renouncing his pro-Confederacy views and advocating for racial equality. As editor, he advocated for blacks to have the right to testify in court. He believed that allowing full civil rights was key to progress, and he represented blacks in court. He subsequently lost his first campaign for Boyle County commonwealth's attorney because of his progressive stances, including saying he would allow black testimony if elected. He remained true to these positions for the remainder of his life.

In 1884, William Breckinridge was elected to the U.S. House of Representatives as a Democrat. His future looked bright. *The Kentucky Encyclopedia* says, "He was recognized as one of his party's chief advocates of free trade and individual rights." According to Klotter, Breckinridge was rumored to be a possible Speaker of the House if the Democrats obtained a majority, the subject of a possible cabinet appointment or even a vice-presidential nominee. He became a sought-after speaker. To say he was prudish, however, would be a great understatement. His pronunciations on morality and women's behavior would prove to be hypocritical. He said in a speech to a Bourbon County women's college: "Chastity is the foundation, the cornerstone of human society and on it rests the foundation of government. Our passions mislead us…[and] pure homes make pure governments."[23] He once said, in a speech before the Oberon Society, as quoted by Klotter, that women must be pure and should avoid "useless hand-shaking, promiscuous kissing, needless touches and all exposures."

Madeline Pollard brought suit against Congressman Breckinridge in 1893, claiming she had been his mistress since 1884, when she was seventeen. She asked for $50,000 in damages. The suit was for breach of promise, claiming he had offered to marry her after his wife's death. Issa, his wife, died in 1892. When the congressman married his third wife, Louise Wing, Pollard brought suit. During the affair, Pollard gave birth to two children. After Issa's death, she had a miscarriage of another. Rumors were spreading about Wing and William, and when confronted by Pollard, he denied them. News broke in the *Cincinnati Commercial Gazette* that Pollard and William Breckinridge were to be married. William Breckinridge denied it after the story was republished in the *Kentucky Leader*.[24] Later, there were rumors that William would marry Wing, and, in fact, he did, on July 18, 1893.

The breach of promise trial captivated America's attention and was covered in newspapers across the nation. According to author Patricia Miller in an interview in *Smithsonian Magazine*, "Pollard was determined to challenge the different standards set out for men and women." In her book *Bringing Down the Colonel*, Miller says, "As chastity becomes central to the definition of a respectable woman in the nineteenth century, women found it was their sexual conduct, not the actions of men, that was really on

Madeline Pollard. *Library of Congress.*

trial." The odds of Pollard winning this case were not good, but she did, and she was awarded $15,000.

Miller argues that the case helped usher in the "transition to a more realistic sexual ethic that flowed in the twentieth century." In Pollard's case, hopefully, she helped change some norms and attitudes of the day. According to Miller, Pollard "really clued people in on how men like Breckinridge were able to get away with having a mistress. There was a real double standard. Women were treated vastly different than men with entirely different consequences on their personal and professional lives."

William ran for reelection in the House in 1894 and, despite serious opposition from various groups, was in a good position to win. Of 19,000 votes cast, he lost by only 255. His political career was over. William Breckinridge would become the editorial writer of his son's *Lexington Morning Herald* paper. According to *The Kentucky Encyclopedia*, from that position, "he led the Gold Democrats against the silver wing of the party, spoke forcibly in 1899 against Democratic gubernatorial candidate William Goebel, and defended railroad interests." He also continued to discuss issues of race. William Breckinridge died in Lexington in 1904 and is buried in Lexington Cemetery.

Pollard had a good life following the trial, settling in Europe, where she met a wealthy widower and was able to travel. She died on December 9, 1945.

3

James W. "Honest Dick" Tate

While James W. Tate was serving as Kentucky state treasurer for twenty years (1868–88), he was a friend and benefactor to all, a genial host at his office and an immensely popular gentleman known as "Colonel Dick" or "Uncle Dick" Tate. However, in 1888, after he absconded with a large chunk of the state treasury, formerly supportive newspapers and his bitter constituents referred to him as "Honest Dick" Tate. For some years after, "Tateism" was an effective cudgel for a politician to use against a rival.

Tate's disappearance from his office, his family, Kentucky and, probably, the United States was a massive shock to the taxpayers and their government. In wall-to-wall coverage of the surprising news in March 1888, the *Courier-Journal* in Louisville captured the astonishment of public officials who worked with Tate, journalists who covered him and people who paid their taxes to him:

> *Like a peal of thunder from a cloudless sky came the announcement this morning that State Treasurer James W. Tate was a defaulter. The amount was variously estimated at from $100,000 to $300,000. A more terrific blow to man's confidence in man could hardly have been dealt. That "Uncle Dick" as he was commonly known—a man reverenced by the people, who delighted in continuing him in a position of trust—had pillaged the public fund was an assertion far too surprising and far too bold for ready belief.*[1]

James "Honest Dick" Tate. *Public domain.*

As it turned out, in his years as treasurer, Tate turned the office into a badly run combination of a cash-advance store, lending institution and personal piggybank. His popularity was built on his eager readiness to extend paycheck advances to state officials or invest in a questionable scheme with political allies.

The story of how Tate achieved and for twenty years maintained his high political office is of course one of money and corruption. But Tate's evolution from kindly "Uncle Dick" to thieving "Honest Dick" also involves hardball political maneuvering and a willingness to blatantly lie and cover up sloppiness and malfeasance over a period of many years.

Throughout his years in Kentucky, Tate led what appeared to be an exemplary life, enriched by a close-knit family, many friends and a successful career. He was born in January 1831, in Franklin County, Kentucky, in the small community of Forks of the Elkhorn, about five miles from downtown Frankfort and the offices Tate would occupy for most of his adult life. His mother, Nancy, was the daughter of Reverend John Taylor, a successful pioneer preacher who helped establish the Baptist Church throughout Kentucky. Tate's father, Colonel Thomas Tate, was a farmer and a veteran of the War of 1812, while his paternal grandfather served in the Virginia Continentals as a soldier in the Revolutionary War.[2] Tate attended school in Franklin and Woodford Counties, and when he was seventeen years old, he got his first job as a clerk at the U.S. Post Office in Frankfort, where his excellent work won him many friends and admirers.

In 1854, Tate got a taste of state political office when Governor Lazarus Powell, Kentucky's first Democratic governor, appointed him as assistant secretary of state. Unfortunately for Tate, a year later, Charles Morehead of the Know-Nothing Party was elected after a campaign in which he exploited native Kentuckians' distrust of German and Irish immigrants who had settled in Louisville, Covington and Lexington. The Know-Nothing campaign culminated on Election Day, August 6, 1855, with the "Bloody Monday" attacks on German and Irish homes and businesses in Louisville. At least twenty-two people were killed.[3]

As a loyal Democrat, Tate decided to leave when the new administration took over, and he moved into "mercantile pursuits" in Frankfort. However, while he was out of government, Tate did not abandon politics. He was active as a member of the Democratic State Central Committee, building strong connections with an organization that years later provided crucial help when he was bucking tradition by repeatedly seeking reelection as state treasurer.

When Governor Beriah Magoffin was elected in 1859, he brought Democrats, including Tate, back into the secretary of state's office. Although Magoffin resigned in 1862 because of conflict with the Kentucky General Assembly over the state's Civil War neutrality, Tate stayed at his post until 1863. Tate supported the John C. Breckinridge, Confederate-sympathizing wing of the Democratic Party, so when Union-sympathizing Thomas Bramlette was elected governor in 1863, Tate again moved out of government and into Frankfort's business community. Tate married in 1856. The couple's three-year-old son died in 1861, and they had a daughter, Edmonia (Mona).[4]

In 1865, Tate was elected assistant clerk of the Kentucky House of Representatives, where he served for two years and solidified his base in the Democratic Party, which would dominate state elections for the next thirty years. At the party's convention in February 1867, Tate was nominated by the Democrats to run for state treasurer, and he won the August general election by more than fifty-four thousand votes.

In the same election, sixty-five-year-old former governor John Helm was ill and unable to campaign but was elected governor again. However, within days of his swearing-in, he died and was succeeded by John W. Stevenson. Tate got a head start on working in the executive branch when Stevenson appointed him to his old job as assistant secretary of state, serving until January 1868, when he began his first two-year term as treasurer. Tate's reputation was such that the brief appointment earned him kudos from the staunchly Democratic *Louisville Daily Journal*, which opined on its front page:

> *The Governor has appointed Mr. James W. Tate Assistant Secretary of State, a position which he held under Governor Powell and Governor Magoffin. It would be superfluous to speak of his qualifications, and quite as idle to mention his merits. He is one of the cleverest gentlemen in Kentucky; and although we know he is the Treasurer-elect of the State and will have to enter on the discharge of the duties of that place at the beginning of next year, still his services to the new administration in his present position will be valuable.[5]*

The next year, the *Journal* would merge with the *Louisville Courier*. Under the guidance of Henry Watterson, the *Courier-Journal* would support Tate and the Democratic Party for decades to come. Like most papers of that era, there was a robust mix of partisan news and opinion on all pages, usually with no byline or name attached to any of the stories.

In early 1871, Governor Stevenson resigned to accept a U.S. Senate seat, and Preston Leslie became governor. Later that year, Leslie ran for a full term as governor, defeating future U.S. Supreme Court Justice John Marshall Harlan. On Leslie's ticket, Tate was elected treasurer for the third time. It was in Leslie's administration that Tate seems to have started his mismanagement of state funds, heading down the trail leading to the corruption that would be his undoing. Apparently, in 1872, Tate began his years-long habit of loaning public money and giving salary advances to his colleagues and friends, including Governor Leslie, who received an advance of $5,000 on a personal note dated July 18, 1872.[6]

In subsequent years, while continuing to buy the goodwill of his political friends and officials who might otherwise exercise some oversight of the treasurer's office, Tate gambled by buying highly speculative stocks and investing in land deals in several states, as well as in coal interests in the eastern Kentucky mountains. He partnered first with the brother of State Auditor Fayette Hewitt in a large amount of Old Mint Spring bourbon and later invested with Auditor Hewitt, as the two state officials tried to profit from a bourbon boom in the 1880s. Of course, this was at a time when Hewitt was supposed to be carefully monitoring the treasurer. Hewitt was later accused of not properly tracking Tate's bookkeeping, but no wrongdoing was proven.[7]

In 1883, Tate joined several of his political friends in starting the *Cincinnati News Journal*, a Democratic newspaper that went out of business in less than a year, running up a debt of $95,556 ($2.4 million in 2020 dollars). Besides Tate, others, including former governor James McCreary and former lieutenant governor John Underwood, the paper's editor, were left holding the bag. (The newspaper's bankruptcy was finalized, and judgment was assessed against Tate and others in February 1888, just a month before he absconded.)[8]

Stories of Tate's profligate spending and his benevolence toward others must have been circulating in the rumor mill that's always been active in state capital cities, certainly including Frankfort. In the 1885 election, Tate was running for his tenth consecutive term, and some Kentuckians were beginning to call for an independent audit of the treasurer's office.

Two newspapers, the *Louisville Commercial* and the *Owensboro Messenger*, were particularly concerned about the rumors of corruption in Tate's office. In February 1885, the *Messenger* favorably cited its Louisville counterpart:

> The Louisville Commercial says "There is no doubt that the treasury has been the prey of rings for so many years that they have come to think they own it. They have fattened on the stealings, have become powerful in the counties and districts, and control the county conventions in the interest of the frauds. They form the Legislatures and control them. They own pretty much, all the earth within the limits of Kentucky.
>
> If the press of the State, which was eager to take up the rumors as to "something wrong," will take up these facts and use them to help in the cause of a Legislature that will have the honesty and the courage to take the thieves by the throat, it can do a service to the cause of good government." The Messenger pledges itself to do whatever is in its power to bring about the result suggested by The Commercial.[9]

In addition to the pressure regarding an audit of his books, Tate was facing political backlash against his repeated runs for office. Prior to adoption of the 1850 constitution, the state treasurer was appointed by the Kentucky General Assembly to a one-year term. New language in the 1850 charter provided that the treasurer would be elected every other year, the only statewide official serving a two-year rather than a four-year term. Clearly, the framers wanted the public to have frequent opportunities to assess the performance of their treasurer.

With Tate's power base in the Democratic Party and the party's dominance in Kentucky politics, if Tate was on the ballot, he would be reelected. In 1885, however, Democratic insiders seemed concerned about Tate's chances of getting the party's nomination. The treasurer's race was the only statewide race on the ballot that year, and the party didn't follow its usual process of choosing its nominee at a party convention. Instead, the party ignored two other potential candidates, and Tate was put on the ballot by the Democratic Central Executive Committee, an organization with which he'd been affiliated for twenty-five years.

There was strong pushback from several newspapers against Tate's power play. Using puns to make a point, an eastern Kentucky paper said: "Dick Tate has been renominated for State Treasurer for about the 100th time. He got the nomination through the State Central Executive Committee, and the reason why they thus dictate to the people is a question they should answer. Such a dictatorial precedent was never before heard of. Dictator anyone else who is a good man satisfies us, but the people ought to dictate a little bit."[10]

In western Kentucky, the *Henderson News* was cited as stating: "Nearly every paper in the State criticizes in strong and terse language the action of the central committee at Frankfort in proclaiming Colonel Dick Tate State Treasurer for another term. The *News* would like to be included in the list of kickers. The colonel is clever enough, but it is hardly probable that offices in Kentucky are hereditary or life long."[11]

When the Republicans declined to nominate a candidate for treasurer in 1885, Tate's only opponent in that year's general election was Judge Fontaine Fox, a Democrat who ran under the banner of the Prohibition Party. Fox attacked Tate and the Democratic Party for "dictating" their nominee to the voters, but he also leveled the first campaign attacks against Tate's management of the treasurer's office. In a speech to hundreds of people at the Daviess County Courthouse, Fox invoked the memory of a longtime state auditor who had embezzled state funds during his twenty-year reign in the 1840s and 1850s and compared that situation to Tate's administration. Fox said:

> We are entitled to an examination of the books. You all remember Mr. Thomas Page and how long he held office. At one time his name was the synonym for honesty and his reputation the standard by which the characters of men were compared. But when his books were examined, he had conducted for a series of years a system of bookkeeping by which he had embezzled an immense sum of money. We must have a look at the books.
>
> Mr. Tate, my opponent, has been selected by a committee of Democrats, and you have been most politely directed to vote for him. This committee acted in this matter regardless of the fact that two other Democrats had been selected and indorsed [sic] in different sections of the State for the same office. Why was the voice and wishes of these sections so plainly and despotically disregarded and held for naught? Was it because this committee did not desire and did not intend that the people of Kentucky should have the man of their choice? Was it because this committee was not ready to have the books examined and laid bare by the new man?[12]

Despite vigorous campaigning by Fox, who would run for governor two years later, Tate was easily reelected in 1885, partly because many Republicans joined Democrats in opposing the Prohibition Party. Although

Fox was defeated, he had asked tough questions about Tate and the Democrats' long hold on state government.

In a post-election analysis, the *Ohio County News* reflected those concerns: "Would it not have been more to *our* interests as citizens and voters to have refused to let those few committeemen dictate Dick Tate to us, and to have voted for and elected Fox, that the books in the Treasury office might have been examined? And were they examined by a new treasurer, might we not have ascertained that there is 'Something rotten in Denmark?'"[13]

In May 1887, Kentucky Democrats convened at Liederkranz Hall in Louisville to nominate their candidates for governor and other statewide offices, including treasurer. Party chairman Samuel Hill knew that the 1885 charges against Tate and other Democrats would again be an issue in the coming campaign, so as he opened the convention, he pushed back hard:

> *"They charge us," Hill said, "with a misappropriation of the revenues of the state. I deny it. They were honestly expended. As evidence of this, the primaries recently held all over the state indorsed* [sic] *a man who has been a State official for 20 years, one who holds the keys to the treasury. I refer to Colonel James W. Tate. Yes, our revenues will increase, and will be expended in the most honorable manner. All may examine our accounts. They will bear the closest scrutiny, and we invite the criticism of our adversaries. Let them pick a flaw if they can. Nowhere will they find an illegal expenditure."*[14]

The convention nominated Tate without opposition, and in what would be his last campaign, he won by twenty thousand votes, a much smaller margin than he had enjoyed in past elections but larger than that of General Simon Bolivar Buckner, the Democrat running for governor at the top of the ticket. A month after the election, Tate paid $5,600 ($152,000 in 2020 dollars) for a house in South Frankfort at the corner of Second and Shelby Streets. Apparently, only Mrs. Tate's name was listed on the deed. A newspaper report of the sale stated, "The Colonel is probably fixing to remain there the rest of his days."[15] In that 1887 gubernatorial race, three candidates, including the Prohibitionist Fox, challenged the Democrats' long hold on power, and all three aggressively campaigned for investigating state offices, particularly the treasurer's office.

Since 1879, Republican nominee William O. Bradley had aggressively attacked Democrats' management of state government. His 1887 platform called for "examination of the state's financial books," which "for nearly

William O. Bradley (*right*), elected governor in 1895. *Library of Congress*.

20 years have been virtually sealed."[16] Bradley lost the 1887 election, but he succeeded in cutting the traditional Democratic margin of victory from about forty thousand votes to sixteen thousand, and eight years later, he was elected governor.[17]

As a result of the "reformist" campaigns of the three non-Democrats in the 1887 race for governor, people calling for an audit of the treasurer's books gained traction. That was reflected in the press for several months after the election. In an article titled "The Clever Fellows," the Owensboro paper once again warned Democrats against complacency and failing to scrutinize the people they were electing and re-electing: "The Democratic party of Kentucky is in a fair way to be destroyed by the 'clever fellows'.... Dick Tate has been re-elected State Treasurer biennially for twenty years, because he is a clever fellow and tells a joke better than anybody, but his books have never been investigated, notwithstanding the scandalous charges repeatedly made."[18] As the Kentucky General Assembly prepared to convene at the end of 1887, "a general sentiment crystallized" with many legislators urging appointment of a commission to examine Tate's records.[19] Although the pressure on Tate was quickly ratcheting up, he still enjoyed a sterling reputation in the capitol and he succeeded in delaying legislative action for several weeks, as he requested time to get the office books in order.

In early 1888, while Tate was clearly attempting to stall the process, Senator John Hendrick, a newly elected legislator who was a former prosecutor, persisted in calling for a legislative investigation. At one point, Tate told Hendrick that several members of Tate's family were sick and that he'd been kept up at night "a great deal" and asked that the investigation be put off so he could better assist the investigators.[20]

At the same time, State Auditor Fayette Hewitt was gently pressing Tate so they could reconcile the state's books, as they were required to do. As the walls seemed to be closing in on Tate, he held on to all cash receipts and deposited only checks in the state's bank account while paying off some of his personal debts.[21]

On Wednesday, March 14, as he was leaving his office, he told several people he had business to transact in Louisville but he would return to the office on Friday in time to post some accounts, which had to be done before his books would balance with Auditor Hewitt's books. The next morning, he took the 8:00 a.m. train to Louisville, and from there he sent Hewitt a letter stating that he was detained in Louisville and would have to cancel their Friday meeting. He also telegraphed his wife that he would be back on Friday night, twenty-four hours later than he originally stated.[22] When

Tate cancelled their Friday meeting, Hewitt was genuinely concerned—Tate had been putting him off for more than a month and recently complained about the legislature's interest in investigating his accounts. On Saturday and Sunday, March 17 and 18, Hewitt set about trying to determine if there was a shortage, and if so, how much was missing.

Through Hewitt's review of books in both offices and discussions with Assistant Treasurer James Hawkins (Tate's brother-in-law), the auditor was able to determine what should have been in the treasury accounts. On Saturday and Sunday, he talked to bankers at Branch Kentucky Bank and Farmers Bank to learn how much the state had in its accounts. From this initial review, Hewitt calculated that there was a discrepancy of $120,841 ($3.3 million in 2020 dollars), and on Monday morning he met with the governor, attorney general and secretary of state.[23] The group met all day and into the evening, collaborating on a report to the legislature that Hewitt wrote. He said that he'd "rather have parted with his right arm than perform that painful duty."[24]

On receiving the report on Tuesday, the members of the Kentucky General Assembly did what legislators will always do in the face of a scandal involving a public official and public money. They spoke out forcefully against the perpetrator and sponsored bills and resolutions to address the problem, all the better to assure their constituents that the sponsors were very concerned, had nothing to do with the scandal or the perpetrator and would make sure it never happens again. They approved Governor Buckner's suspension of Tate, authorized Buckner to offer a $5,000 reward for Tate's apprehension and conviction and appointed a committee to draft articles of impeachment against Tate, so that he could be permanently removed from office.

The next morning, when the Franklin circuit clerk opened his office, he was met by Attorney General P. Wat Hardin filing a lawsuit against Tate, asking for "at least $175,000" and seizure of all of Tate's property.[25] Of course, by the time these officials were able to act against Tate, he was probably in Canada. After he left Frankfort (without luggage, according to one report), he spent two nights in Louisville, staying (as he always did) at the Louisville Hotel, and took in a Thursday night show at Macauley's Theater. On Friday, he went with a friend to Wanamaker & Brown's, a clothing store at the corner of Fourth and Jefferson, where he bought three shirts. While he spent most of Friday at the hotel, several people saw him at Louis Seelbach's Bar & Grill, then located at the corner of Sixth and Main.

After his Saturday midday meal at the hotel, he paid his bill and caught the 2:30 p.m. train to Cincinnati. John Pye, who knew Tate and was on the train with him, said Tate seemed "preoccupied…moody and reserved [and] not in his usual good humor."[26] Pye said Tate hurriedly left the station in Cincinnati, and that was apparently the last time he was seen in or near Kentucky. The Owensboro paper reported that before he left Louisville, he sent his wife by express $2,500, but "in marked contrast to the conduct of her guilty husband, she promptly turned the money over to his bondsmen."[27]

Back in Frankfort, the chaos was kicking in. The atmosphere "was such that almost everybody was under suspicion, either as an accomplice of Tate or because of owing the Treasury money, and those who had borrowed money from the Treasury were numerous."[28]

During Tate's impeachment trial in the Senate, Auditor Hewitt testified that his most recent estimate of the shortage in the state accounts was $197,964, but he said that could increase or decrease as checks came in or were cashed. Henry Murray, one of Hewitt's assistants, testified that on Tate's last day in the office, Murray saw Tate put "an unusually large roll of money" in his pocket, along with a "plush coin purse filled with gold." Tate also had "two half-pound tobacco sacks filled with gold coin," but Murray didn't know what Tate did with those.[29]

Tate's record keeping was so haphazard and indecipherable that it was difficult to determine the exact amount of money Tate had stolen and misallocated. Within weeks of Tate's disappearance, a review by legislative investigators put the total at $247,000 ($6.7 million in 2020 dollars), a number that has been etched in history as the tale of Tate has been told for over 130 years. Fortunately, the state was able to claw back a portion of the losses by selling Tate's personal assets (eventually amounting to $100,000) and recovering on some of the IOUs and other delinquent accounts. A commission appointed by the governor reported in 1890 that the "actual defalcation" was closer to $150,000 and could be "much less."[30]

In 1895, when the state lost the last lawsuit against several of Tate's bondsmen, it was reported that the state had earlier recovered $26,000 from some of the other bondsmen. In the end, the amount lost may have been around $100,000, which could be close to the amount of cash that Tate made off with when he boarded the train to Louisville.[31] Regardless of the amount of the defalcation, Tate's case had a significant impact on Kentucky law and politics. When the Kentucky Constitutional Convention met in 1890, the drafters of the revised constitution made sure to prohibit state officeholders from seeking reelection to the same office after serving a four-year term. The officeholders limited in this manner started at the top with the governor and included all the others,

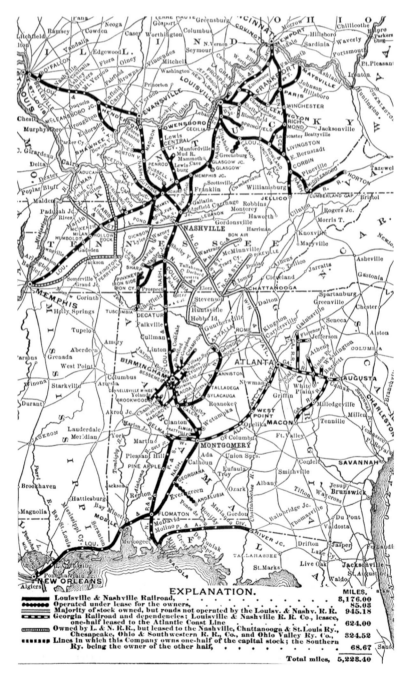

1901 Poor's *Manual of Railroads of the United States.* Louisville & Nashville Railroad. *Public domain.*

was an effective legislator who pushed for many reforms that were not popular with some of his conservative Democratic colleagues. His battles with corporations included working for regulation of banks, elimination of toll roads and limitations on the use of state prison labor. He fought for better public education, civil rights for blacks, the right to vote for women (at least in school board races) and the right for women to serve as members of local school boards. Voters liked his reform agenda, but some in his own party never did.[6]

One of his early legislative priorities was reducing the tolls that had to be paid by his constituents who used the Lexington Turnpike and other area toll roads and bridges, including the Roebling Bridge to Cincinnati. When the legislation passed, Goebel made an enemy in John L. Sandford, a Covington banker who was president of the Lexington Turnpike Company that collected the tolls.[7] Goebel and Sandford clashed again when Sandford blocked Goebel's effort to become a judge on the Kentucky Court of Appeals. Goebel retaliated by shepherding a bill through the legislature allowing city, county and school district deposits to be moved from Sandford's bank to another Covington bank. At that point, the quick-tempered Sandford stated that he was "going to kill Goebel or be killed."[8]

Indeed, not long after Goebel published an anonymous newspaper article calling Sandford "Colonel John Gonorrhea Sandford," Goebel and Sandford met on the street in Covington. Goebel acknowledged that he had written the article, and the two men drew their pistols and fired at each other. Sandford was fatally wounded by Goebel's shot, while Sandford's shot missed its mark. Goebel was not charged in the shooting when he said he had acted in self-defense; Goebel and witnesses said Sandford fired first.

Sandford was a former Confederate Civil War officer, so he had many friends and allies in business and politics. There is no doubt the Sandford shooting added names to the list of Goebel's enemies as he continued to ascend the political ladder. He garnered more opponents when he backed a controversial bill in the 1898 general assembly. Goebel questioned Kentucky's election process after the election of two Republicans, Governor William O. Bradley in 1895 and President William McKinley in 1896. His concerns motivated Goebel to push the "Goebel Election Law," enacted in 1898 after he became senate president pro tem.

The new law created a three-member Board of Election Commission, which chose people in every county who would review and rule on election results. Under the law, the commissioners would be appointed by the Kentucky General Assembly, which was dominated by Democrats, so

Republicans saw it as totally corrupt while Democrats characterized it as reform. The bill passed with a straight party line vote but was vetoed by Governor Bradley. The veto was overridden in each legislative chamber by the majority Democrats. It was probably unfortunate for Goebel's political prospects, as it is likely that many Kentuckians saw the law as a heavy-handed and hyper-partisan effort by Goebel to steal future elections.

The 1895 gubernatorial election of Republican Bradley over a divided Democratic Party signaled the end of the thirty-year dominance of the post–Civil War conservative Democrats. However, Bradley could not seek reelection in 1899, so the field was wide open, and several candidates stepped forward, including Goebel, the top Democrat in the general assembly. The other Democrats were former Kentucky attorney general P. Wat Hardin and former congressman William J. Stone. After a raucous six-day nominating convention at the Music Hall in downtown Louisville, Goebel emerged with the nomination on the twenty-sixth ballot. Goebel's conduct and maneuverings during the convention, while successful in securing him the nomination, turned more voters against him, but he believed he could win them back with a campaign against the L&N and other corporations.[9]

At the Republican convention in Lexington, Attorney General William S. Taylor was nominated, despite a lack of support from Bradley. In his time as governor, Bradley had reached out to black voters, but Taylor was interested in disassociating the party from "Black Republicanism." When black leaders at the convention threatened to bolt, Taylor tried to maintain party unity by promising that his administration would include blacks in high state jobs.[10]

Taylor and Goebel were soon joined in the race by another candidate. The "Honest Election Democrats," unhappy with the conduct and outcome of the Music Hall Convention, nominated former governor John Y. Brown. The general election campaign started in August. Although it was short in duration, it proved long on drama. Taylor and the Republicans embraced President McKinley's administration and warned about the "desperate character" of Goebel and the likelihood of election fraud.[11]

Goebel campaigned with relentless attacks on his old adversary, the L&N Railroad. In a speech in Mayfield, he said the "issue that transcends the others is whether the trusts or the people shall rule…whether the Louisville and Nashville Railroad Company is the servant or the master of the people of this Commonwealth."[12] In rural Kentucky, the crowds usually responded enthusiastically with "Servant!" In Danville, Goebel said, "I believe the railroad corporations should have a bit in their mouths and the Democratic Party should hold the bridle."[13]

To bolster its influence and lobbying efforts, the L&N frequently made campaign contributions, but it was particularly aggressive in its efforts to stop Goebel. Several years after the 1899 election, August Belmont (chairman of L&N's board of directors) admitted that he and his associates had spent more than $500,000 to defeat Goebel and added, "We would have spent twice that much had we thought it necessary."[14]

Knowing he needed a campaign boost, Goebel invited the popular orator and 1896 presidential candidate William Jennings Bryan to campaign with him in a barnstorming tour across the state. Eyeing a second presidential run in 1900, the populist Democrat agreed to come to Kentucky. Goebel and Bryan traveled by train for three days from western Kentucky to Covington, stopping frequently along the way. The *Louisville Courier-Journal*, which was all in for Goebel, gave extensive coverage to the tour and estimated that 150,000 people heard Bryan give an "unqualified indorsement" to the Goebel ticket.[15] After the Bryan tour, Goebel's friends were "wild with enthusiasm," and the *Kentucky Gazette* stated, "There seems to be little doubt of his election now!"[16]

In the final days before the vote, Goebel and Taylor campaigned in Louisville, and there was an expectation that Election Day would see violence and fraud. Under the headline "Bayonet Rule," the *Courier-Journal* reported that "for the first time in the history of Kentucky, the Governor has ordered out troops to participate in an election….City authorities and Democratic leaders say that the Governor's plain intention in the desperate straits to which his party has been driven by a knowledge of their certain defeat, is to seek to control the election here by force of arms."[17] The Democratic mayor of Louisville deployed five hundred private police officers, ostensibly to keep the peace, but perhaps to intimidate Republicans.[18]

Despite the concerns, Election Day, November 7, 1899, was relatively peaceful across the commonwealth. On election night, both sides claimed victory. Goebel had a slight lead, but votes from the Republican counties in the mountains were slow to come in. A few days later, when the counting was through, Taylor had 193,714 votes to 191,331 for Goebel. Former governor Brown picked up 12,040, probably depriving Goebel of Democratic votes that could have been the difference in such a close race.

The election results had to be certified by the three-member Board of Election Commission, created the year before by the Goebel Election Law, appointed by the Kentucky General Assembly and considered to be controlled by Goebel. There were charges and countercharges of election fraud, vote stealing and other irregularities that the board might have to resolve. However, the board was not scheduled to meet until two weeks following the election. In that interim, between five hundred and one thousand armed men from the mountains of eastern Kentucky made their way to Frankfort. Most were recruited by Republican Caleb Powers, the young Knox County school superintendent who had just been elected secretary of state on the ticket with Taylor. It was generally thought the men rode free of charge to the capital city on trains provided by the L&N, which was still fighting to defeat Goebel. Tensions eased a bit when the commission met and, surprisingly, voted two to one to certify Taylor's victory.[19]

On December 12, Taylor was inaugurated, and although the election campaign had been bitterly contested for months, Goebel seemed to gracefully accept the result, thanked his supporters and said he was heading to Arizona to rest and visit his brother. Some of his supporters remained convinced the election was stolen, and despite Goebel's reluctance, the Democratic State Executive Committee urged him and his running mate, J.C.W. Beckham, to contest the election in the Kentucky General Assembly, which was still controlled by their party and which had the constitutional authority to decide a contested election. Finally, Goebel agreed to file an election contest, and legislative leaders said a select committee would be appointed to investigate the allegations of wrongdoing. Once again, mountain Republicans picked up their weapons and headed for the capitol, determined to protect what they viewed as their candidate's victory. Armed conflict and even civil war seemed possible.[20]

On January 2, 1900, the first day of the Kentucky General Assembly session, Goebel formally challenged Taylor's November victory by filing an election contest. The next day, a contest committee was appointed to investigate Goebel's allegations, including vote fraud in eastern Kentucky, illegal election activities by the L&N Railroad and intimidation of voters by the troops who had been called out by Governor Bradley. Unfortunately, tensions were heightened when the "random selection" of the eleven committee members resulted in ten Democrats and one Republican being selected, probably confirming Republican concerns that the election would be taken from Taylor and handed to Goebel.

When the contest proceedings began on January 15 in a ballroom at Frankfort's Capital Hotel, the *Courier-Journal* reported that "the advance guard of 2,000 to 3,000 Republican 'witnesses' from the eastern Kentucky mountains have arrived in the capital city and the streets are filled with them." The paper said some of the men were wearing army coats and "are known to be members of the military companies in the mountains." Several hundred partisans attended the contest proceedings, which at one point were interrupted by an unusual clatter at the rear of the hall. On investigation, it was found that one hundred rounds of no. 2 buckshot had rolled out of the pocket of the overcoat of a man who carried his coat on his arm.[21]

The next day, in the crowded lobby of the same hotel, three men were killed and three wounded in a "pistol encounter" while legislators and state officials looked on. The *Courier-Journal* said the encounter had caused much excitement "because the public was already so on the tiptoe of expectancy on account of Republican threats of riot that every man's first thought was: 'Riot is on, and what will be the end?'"[22]

On January 23, as armed men from eastern Kentucky continued to arrive in Frankfort, there were reports that Governor Taylor might attempt to dissolve the legislature while the election contest was pending or forcibly resist an adverse decision by the general assembly. In response, General Joseph H. Lewis, recently retired chief justice of the Kentucky Court of Appeals, issued a statement supporting the constitutionality of the election contest and opining that if the contest was decided in Goebel's favor, he would be the legal governor and Taylor would be powerless to do any official act and "not entitled to official recognition by any civil officer or soldier." Lewis concluded his statement by asking, "What then would be the result of the threatened forcible resistance to a decision favorable to Goebel? There might be rioting and bloodshed. But if a soldier should, under order of Taylor, claiming to be Governor, kill a peace officer or citizen, he would be guilty of murder; for the law would require him to know Goebel, not Taylor, was the legal Governor."[23]

Lewis's advocacy for the rule of law probably fell on deaf ears among the hundreds of men who were camping out for days on the capitol grounds in downtown Frankfort. One of the allegations in Goebel's election contest was that ballots used in many eastern Kentucky counties were recorded on "tissue paper" and should be declared invalid. Republican leaders initially encouraged the mountaineers to come to Frankfort as witnesses in the contest proceedings, but many of them came "armed with standard equipment of a Kentucky gentleman of that time, a .44 Colt revolver, a Winchester rifle, a jug of corn liquor and a pack of cards." The *Courier-Journal* reported that the men came from Bell, Clay, Harlan, Knox, Laurel, Rockcastle and Whitley Counties. Historian Thomas D. Clark later wrote, "These wild drunken mountaineers were carried [by the L&N Railroad] to the Capitol on the pretense of protecting their democratic rights to a free franchise; truly they were carried there for the purpose of intimidating a recalcitrant General Assembly in its recount of the votes of the November election."[24]

On Monday, January 29, Governor Taylor notified the Kentucky General Assembly that he would not hand over his certificate of election, as requested by the legislators. That night, as the contest proceedings were expected to wrap up within a day or so, it was reported that "the railroad lobby is demanding of the Republican leaders that force be resorted to, because they prefer that almost anything should happen rather than see Senator Goebel installed as Governor." When the contest board adjourned later, about fifty of the mountain men assembled at the door of the meeting room and "threats were made against Mr. Aaron Kohn," one of Goebel's attorneys.[25]

It was in this atmosphere of high tension and proliferation of weapons around the capitol that John Hendrick, an attorney and friend of Goebel's, advised Goebel to take precautions against an attack. "I want you to promise me you will not go out of the hotel again," Hendrick said. "They will assassinate you." Goebel was reported to have replied, "If they assassinate me, my death will be to the Democratic Party of Kentucky what the blowing up of the *Maine* was to Cuba."[26]

On the morning of Tuesday, January 30, heading for the Senate for the 11:00 a.m. convening, Goebel left the Capital Hotel with Jack Chinn and Eph Lillard and walked the two blocks across the railroad tracks and up Broadway to the Kentucky State Capitol. The capitol grounds were quiet, as the armed encampment had mostly dispersed, either gone home or to nearby rooming houses. As Lillard walked ahead, Goebel and Chinn walked past the ornate fountain in front of the capitol. A shot was fired from the Executive Office Building to Goebel's right. Chinn said he heard the report of a rifle, and Goebel bent double, groaned, clutched his right side and fell to his knees. "My God! Goebel, they have killed you," Chinn said. "I guess they have," Goebel said as he fell.[27]

Bleeding profusely, Goebel was carried back to his hotel, where he was met by Dr. E.E. Hume, who later said he knew immediately that Goebel was fatally wounded. A small rifle bullet had entered Goebel's right breast and exited his back near his spine. That night, Governor Taylor declared a state of emergency and ordered the militia to Frankfort. He cited a "state of insurrection" and ordered the legislature to adjourn immediately and meet the following week in London, the county seat of heavily Republican Laurel County, over one hundred miles from Frankfort.

Ignoring Taylor's declaration, legislative Democrats the next day attempted to meet, but the capitol was blocked by state militia, as were the

Opera House, Frankfort City Hall and the Franklin County Courthouse. The legislators tried twice to meet in the streets of downtown Frankfort, but the soldiers dispersed them. Finally, they were able to assemble secretly at the Capital Hotel, and with Goebel mortally wounded in a room two floors above them, a quorum of the Kentucky Senate and House accepted the reports of the contest committee and declared that Goebel and Beckham had won the election and should be seated as governor and lieutenant governor. The two men were sworn in immediately, and Goebel's first and only act as governor was to sign a proclamation disbanding the state guards and sending them home.[28]

Kentucky appeared to have two governors, as Republicans refused to acknowledge the legality of the actions by the legislative Democrats. Then, on Saturday, February 3, Goebel died at 6:45 p.m. Within an hour, Beckham took the oath of office and became governor. Three days later, several leading Republicans and Democrats met in Louisville and signed an agreement under which Taylor would resign and bring a peaceful resolution to the standoff. However, Taylor was having none of it and wanted the courts to resolve the question of who was governor.

When the Kentucky Court of Appeals sided with the general assembly and determined that Goebel and Beckham were legally elected, affirming Beckham as governor, Taylor appealed to the U.S. Supreme Court. After hearing oral arguments on April 30 and May 1, the justices ruled on May 21, 1900, dismissing the case and holding that Kentucky's highest court had correctly decided that the courts had no power to interfere with the determination of the general assembly in an election contest.[29] The Supreme Court's decision brought some order to Kentucky's chaotic political landscape. A special gubernatorial election was scheduled for November. Beckham won by a narrow margin and was elected to a full term in 1903.

While Taylor's case was moving through the courts, criminal charges were brought against several people for conspiring to assassinate Goebel. Evidence was developed that indicated the fatal bullet came from a .38-caliber rifle fired from a window in the office of Secretary of State Caleb Powers. When a warrant was issued for Powers's arrest, he tried to flee Frankfort but was apprehended. After testimony from a state employee alleging a conspiracy to kill Goebel, a Franklin County grand jury indicted Taylor, Powers and several others for their participation in the alleged plot. When he was indicted, Taylor fled to Indianapolis to avoid trial. The Indiana governor refused to extradite him back to Kentucky, so Taylor lived the rest of his life working as a lawyer in Indianapolis.

Left: Memorial engraving of Governor William Goebel. *Library of Congress.*

Right: Grave of William Goebel, Frankfort Cemetery. *Photo by Robert Schrage.*

At Powers's trial, there was testimony that his brother was overheard saying, "Goebel is to be killed today" before he admitted a stranger into Powers's office on the morning of the shooting. When Powers testified on his own behalf, he admitted that he had organized the Frankfort gathering of the armed eastern Kentuckians but claimed it was done to protect Taylor and not to assault Goebel or other Democrats. The jury briefly deliberated then convicted Powers.

After appeals, Powers was tried twice more, leading to a conviction and, in the third trial, a hung jury. In 1908, while awaiting his fourth trial, he was pardoned by Republican governor Augustus Willson. The next year, Willson pardoned Taylor, along with Jim Howard, who had been convicted of traveling to Frankfort from Clay County on the morning of the shooting, getting off the train, walking to the capitol to meet with Powers and then firing the fatal shot.

Powers was later elected to Congress four times, serving in the U.S. House of Representatives from 1911 to 1919. He was a delegate to the 1912 Republican National Convention, which nominated President William Howard Taft over former President Theodore Roosevelt.

gambling and mob influences, many local officials turned a blind eye to corruption and illegal activity. In a description by the publisher of the book *Bossism and Reform in a Southern City: Lexington, Kentucky, 1880–1940* by James Duane Bolin, Klair is described in a manner befitting most political bosses: "As a political boss and a practitioner of what George Washington Plunkitt of Tammany Hall referred to as 'honest graft,' Klair applied lessons of organization, innovation, manipulation, power, and control from the machine age to bring together diverse groups of Lexingtonians and Kentuckians as supporters of a powerful political machine." He also brought a lot of money to his business from state contracts.

In Frankfort, William "Percy" Haly had statewide influence and was a crony of William Goebel. George "Boss" Cox in Cincinnati was one of the most famous politicos in the nation. Primary support for the bosses came from poor people and, to a lesser extent, from members of the middle class. According to William Shannon in his June 1969 *American Heritage Magazine* article "The Political Machine I: Rise and Fall the Age of the Bosses," "[It] was the poorest and most insecure who provided the boss with the base of his political power. Their only strength, as Professor Richard C. Wade of the University of Chicago has observed, was in their numbers."

All the political bosses in Kentucky, except Galvin, were Democrats, many were raised poor and most were Catholic. In Kentucky, bosses were "kingmakers" and ruled for about fifty years. Looking back, bosses are often seen in a negative light, but they are an important part of both Kentucky and American history. Some argue that the bosses helped government deliver services effectively. The bosses existed in a time of tremendous growth and development, but there was also disenfranchisement, poverty and corruption. Only a reform movement that incrementally grew over decades would rid the nation of these historic figures who controlled so much of the political landscape.

The most significant political bosses in Kentucky were in Louisville, where John Henry Whallen controlled the city and was joined by his brother James Patrick. On the state level, former congressman Ben Johnson was the most powerful official in Kentucky and developed a political machine at the Kentucky Highway Commission, controlling funds and projects based on loyalty.

The Whallen Brothers

According to author and University of Kentucky history professor Tracy Campbell, "Louisville holds a unique place in the history of American election fraud, and in the early twentieth century democracy was systematically subverted there on an annual basis."[2] Louisville became the first city in the United States to use the secret ballot, commonly referred to as the "Australian ballot." Before the secret ballot was adopted, "partisan newspapers printed filled-out ballots which party workers distributed on election day so voters could drop them directly in boxes."[3] Across America, the secret ballot was common by 1892, but paying people to vote was outlawed only in 1925.

The secret ballot was instituted in Louisville because of the fraudulent election of 1887, when the mayoral race was, according to *Louisville Courier Journal* editor Henry Watterson, "without parallel in the history of Louisville fraud and corruption." It was discovered that the names of candidates on poll books were so close together that "corrupt clerks could place a mark in the wrong column without being easily detected."[4] A commission called the Commonwealth Club was a self-appointed group that responded to the election fraud. One member was State Representative Arthur Wallace, who researched whether the Australian ballot could legally be used in Kentucky and found that it could be. As Campbell says, "It quietly became law in February, 1888" and was first used that December. However, the new secret ballot had little impact on voter corruption, and the Whallen brothers flourished.

John Henry Whallen was born in May 1850 in New Orleans, and his family settled in Maysville, Kentucky, and later in Cincinnati, Ohio. When he was a boy, John served in the Confederate army and was at one point a scout for General John Hunt Morgan. He moved to Louisville following the Civil War. In 1880, he and his brother James opened the Buckingham Theater. Both brothers were founders of the Empire Circuit, a syndicate of burlesque theaters. According to Karen Gray and Sarah Yates in *The Kentucky Encyclopedia*, "The Whallens' theater interests meshed with political ones, and the Buckingham Theater's Green Room became the reputed hub of local Democratic politics, with John Whallen as the 'Buckingham Boss.'"[5] The Whallens worked so closely together at the Buckingham that the *Kentucky Irish American Newspaper* said, "When the Whallen boys buy a pair of shoes, one belongs to Jim and the other to John."[6]

John was unsuccessful in marriage, having been wed three times, but he was successful in business. He listed himself in the 1900 census as a

Left: John Whallen. *Right*: James Whallen. *Public domain*.

"capitalist." The two brothers were active in business, including the whiskey trade. Around 1902, they created their own wholesale and retail business. Their most profitable brand was Spring Bank Whiskey. However, their most profitable business was the theater, especially when they switched from legitimate shows to burlesque.

According to the blog at pre-prowhiskeymen.blogspot.com posted by Jack Sullivan:

> [It] *was neither rectified whiskey nor phony medicinals…that thrust the Whallens into the political arena. It was the need to protect their entertainment business—having abandoned serious theater for shows featuring scantily clad women who provided "female companionship" and off-stage services to male patrons. Although the Whallens gave free passes to members of the Louisville police force and usually were repaid with a blind eye, in 1880 an undercover police taskforce raided the Buckingham Theater and closed down a production called Female Bathers in the Sea. A Louisville grand jury of thirteen men, all workers or unemployed were unimpressed by the evidence, however, and refused to indict the Whallens on a charge of obscenity.*

Over the years, there were many tactics used by the Whallen Machine to achieve its fraudulent election goals. In one election, it established "house to house" voting, in which voters were required to be at home over a two-night period in order to vote. Once, the Whallens used a portable voting station—the voting machine was placed on a train near the convergence of the Eleventh and Twelfth Wards. In this case, they feared a large contingent of anti-Whallen voters at this location, so they moved the train when heavy lines formed to vote.

In 1899, John (with the concurrence of the Democratic Party) completely annulled a primary election when the machine candidates seemed to be losing. Giving out cash to buy votes and tampering with registration rolls was commonplace. Ironically, one person paying cash for the machine was Arthur Wallace, who advocated for the Australian ballot. Campbell writes police intimidation of voters and registrants was also an often-used tactic of the Whallen brothers.

However, it was in the 1905 mayoral election that Boss Whallen went too far over the top on election fraud. He had been orchestrating fraudulent elections for more than a decade, and by 1905, the corruption was open and rampant. However, the massive corruption in that election may have set the stage for the beginning of the end of the Whallen Machine, as Louisville saw the rise of the "Fusionist" Party, a group of Democrats and Republicans who wanted to end Whallen's control of city politics.

The voter rolls were full of fraudulent names, and the machine focused on getting the vote out. The machine's candidate was Paul Barth, while Joseph O'Neal was the Fusionist candidate. Voters were intimidated with threats by the police, some violence took place and money was paid to persuade people not to register. African Americans who would most likely vote against the machine faced significant intimidation during the campaign.

According to Campbell, the 1905 election showed the importance of money in politics, especially when it was used in widespread vote buying. He writes: "Bank records revealed that the Democratic campaign fund had deposits of over $69,000 between August 31, 1905 and election day in early November, nearly three times the amount of the Fusionist Fund. Furthermore, those records show that during registration week in early October, $22,290 was removed from the account and on election day another $23,360 was removed from the account."[7]

The political money was raised primarily from city employees, common practice in boss machine cities. According to Fred Bishop, treasurer of the Democratic campaign fund, most of the money was spent on election tampering. On election eve, Bishop said some precinct campaigns came in for more money, and it was distributed, no questions asked. Some of the money went to pay police and fire personnel to take Election Day off and help with Democratic chores. Campbell says that more than 20 percent of the firefighters claimed they were sick on Election Day.

Election officers were supposed to be neutral. According to Campbell, in 1905, 89 percent of the 356 election officers worked for the city or the county or had relatives who worked for local government.

The night before the election, ten thousand people showed up at the courthouse to support Fusionist candidates. The police walked through the crowd, writing down names. The

Paul Barth. *Public domain.*

Evening Post reported that each police officer was expected to register phantom voters, using their own addresses. There were 313 illegally registered voters from the homes of police and firefighters for this election.[8] On Election Day, certain precincts did not have enough ballots, and in others, voters were turned away. In one case, a voting station didn't open until noon. One ballot box was taken by armed men. In others, the machine would use skullduggery to slow down voting, allowing fewer people to vote.

The final tally indicated that Democrat Barth beat Fusionist O'Neal 19,645 to 16,557. A post-election investigation showed that "at least 790 illegal registrants had voted." Testimony during the investigation exposed extensive voter fraud, especially in the Twelfth Ward, where "830 properly registered voters tried to vote but were unable to, because no ballots had been supplied."[9]

A court challenge was initiated, but the Jefferson Chancery Court ruled two to one against overturning the election. As the new mayor, Barth ran the city in typical boss fashion. However, in a very surprising vote, the Kentucky Court of Appeals overturned the election by a vote of four to two, agreeing with the Fusionists that there was "overwhelming evidence of illegal registrations." The court held that 6,292 voters were disenfranchised, enough to overturn the election results.[10] The court ordered all municipal offices vacated and directed Governor Beckham to appoint a new mayor. He chose Robert W. Bingham, and the Republicans won a special election in the fall to complete Barth's term. Paul Barth would kill himself in 1907, it is said in part because of the way he was treated after a small scandal. It

Political cartoon of Paul Barth. *Public domain.*

Left: Whallen brothers' grave, Louisville, Kentucky. *Photo by Robert Schrage*.

Below: Buckingham Theater (Savoy), Louisville, Kentucky. *Public domain*.

involved his purchasing a costly saddle horse for transportation in the city, for which he was taunted.

Was the Whallen Machine dead? The next regular election was to be held in 1909. Whallen could not use his old tactics, as there was extensive scrutiny of his activities. Instead, he ran a very racist campaign, utilizing "white supremacy" and hitting the issue hard. Whallen's candidate and the machine won. Mayor Bingham said, "With the return of the old corrupt and vicious Democratic ring…conditions here now are as bad, if not worse, than they had ever been." John Whallen died in 1913, and his grand funeral procession included over one hundred carriages and Arthur Wallace as a pallbearer. James Whallen took over the reins after his brother's death, and the machine rolled on until he died in 1930, ending the long run of the Whallen Machine.

The Whallens controlled Louisville's city hall for decades and did so without many adverse consequences. However, fraud did cause the Kentucky Court of Appeals to throw out the results of three elections (1905, 1923 and 1925) orchestrated by the machine. For the most part, the Whallens were never held accountable for the fraud, and both John and James lived out their lives free of indictments, court cases or jail time. Like most cities, Louisville eventually shook off the machine bosses and implemented significant reforms.

Ben Johnson and the Highway Commission

Ben Johnson is certainly a colorful figure in a long list of interesting and provocative politicians throughout Kentucky history. He was born on May 20, 1858, and grew up during the turbulent times of the Civil War and its aftermath. His father, William, was a state senator and served as acting lieutenant governor. Ben Johnson once killed a man in 1880 in an Election Day fight and exchanged shots with others on at least one occasion.[11] He carried a pistol during his entire life, including when he served as a member of Congress.

Johnson was widely viewed as a generous man, and he made a fortune as a businessman, banker and attorney. He entered politics, first in Bardstown, his hometown, and then in the state legislature. Not even thirty years old, he became Speaker of the Kentucky House of Representatives. President

Cleveland appointed Johnson internal revenue collector for Kentucky's Fifth District, allowing him to give out political patronage jobs. According to Klotter, "Throughout his life, he firmly believed in rewarding allies and dealing ruthlessly with enemies."[12] After serving for one year as a state senator, Johnson was elected to the U.S. Congress, where he served from 1907 to 1927. He briefly campaigned for a gubernatorial nomination in 1911 but withdrew because of significant opposition to his Catholicism.

According to Harrison, Johnson was "determined to become Boss Ben" and "the power behind the gubernatorial throne." In 1927, at age sixty-nine, he left Congress and appeared ready to settle into retirement. However, his biggest role, the one for which he would become best known, was still ahead. As a strong partisan, Johnson was concerned about the factionalism in Kentucky politics. He also had a strong dislike for former governor and current U.S. senator J.C.W. Beckham.

Democratic governor William J. Fields asked Johnson to become chairman of the Kentucky Highway Commission, a very powerful position. Johnson initially declined, but he eventually accepted. His acceptance established his dominance over Kentucky's highway projects, and he became Boss Ben. With the passage of the Highway Act of 1921, expenditures for road projects increased tremendously. Historians James Klotter and John Muir write:

> *The resulting transformation of southern life gave rural people a mobility, a freedom, a release they had never before experienced. An erosion of provincial isolation, an improvement in school bus routes and an increased labor mobility all had resulted. Kentucky had felt these changes and by 1927 devoted over two-fifths of its $28,400,000 budget to roads. With funds like that available, with control over a large work force, the highway commission could be a source of vast political patronage, power and corruption or a positive force for betterment of Kentucky life.*[13]

In office, Johnson would use power and patronage to his full advantage. Klotter and Muir point out what newspapermen and others said: "[Johnson] never forgets a friend—and he also sometimes remembers an enemy.…[H]e could conceive more political reprisals and execute them with greater personal delight than any other man I have known…he would do almost anything for you if he liked you, but would destroy you if he didn't [and] there were few on the other side whom 'Old Ben' liked."[14]

Johnson jumped almost immediately into gubernatorial politics, opposing his old enemy Beckham in the 1927 election. He supported Republican Flem

Ben Johnson. *Library of Congress.*

Left: Ben Johnson as an older man. *Public domain*. *Right*: Governor J.C.W. Beckham. *Library of Congress*.

Sampson, who won. Johnson used his power to full advantage. Sampson began creating his own political machine and gave extensive authority to the state's highway engineer, J.S. Watkins, who subsequently asked all employees to list their "political, religious, and fraternal ties."[15] When employees were fired, Johnson offered to resign, but Sampson refused his offer. However, in December 1929, he did dismiss Johnson, but the Democratic attorney general ordered the firing reversed, since Johnson still had time left in his term. Later, the court of appeals upheld the firing, and Johnson was out of his position.

Johnson went after Sampson, and the legislature passed a bill reforming the commission, facilitating Johnson's return. By 1930, Johnson was back on the commission and was quickly named chair. He transformed himself into a "dictator,"[16] something he hated in the Republican administration. A stickler for detail, Johnson had complete control over all operations. In two fiscal years, Johnson's commission would spend over $30 million, and he and his allies made all the decisions on how to spend the money.

According to Klotter and Muir, "Johnson believed in the spoils system and saw nothing wrong in rewarding one's friends." They say that one standard practice by Johnson was to deposit state funds of up to $25,000 in local banks of his choice and then withdraw the funds at a later date for road projects. The banks had use of those funds until that occurred. Also, many road projects were promised to legislators to get the reform bill passed. Johnson went about paying these debts.

During this time, roads were built for political purposes. They were often disconnected, giving Kentucky the nickname the "Detour State." He was all-powerful, and one of the biggest mistakes any official could make was to be disloyal to him. It was reported that he had as many as ten thousand road workers and their families "all ready to do his bidding." If not, they would be fired. It was reported that a contribution of two percent of salary from workers was required to support Democratic candidates.[17] Ben Johnson controlled so many positions, and at the local level projects meant construction jobs and a lot of economic activity. "Johnson only wanted two things—loyalty and votes."[18]

Johnson wanted to be the power broker in Kentucky's gubernatorial politics. He supported Ruby Laffoon for governor in the 1931 election and was instrumental in getting A.B. "Happy" Chandler on the ticket as lieutenant governor. He arranged that with the help of his son-in-law J. Dan Talbott, an up-and-comer who was nominated for auditor. Laffoon won easily, and the election was a victory for Johnson, who was secure in his position as Kentucky Highway Commission chair.

Governor Happy Chandler. *Kenton County Library*.

Johnson often had disagreements, even with the governors he helped put into office. Johnson and Laffoon disagreed over Laffoon's call for a state sales tax. Issues related to patronage also affected their relationship, and Laffoon reined Johnson in by requiring that all contracts and supply purchases be approved by the governor's office. As their differences continued, Johnson became active in anti-Laffoon factions. The governor fired Johnson on January 7, 1935. The question being asked was, "Is Ben Johnson done politically?" He had a way of coming back from the political graveyard.

In the 1935 election for governor, Johnson supported the charismatic Chandler, who won easily. Ben Johnson would be back. J. Dan Talbott became Chandler's chief advisor, but Talbott and Johnson had a falling out. In less than eight months, Johnson was out again, ending forever the power of this unique Kentucky boss.

Johnson lived until June 4, 1950, and was often bitter during the years following the end of his political career. He is buried in Saint Joseph's Cemetery in Bardstown.

Conclusion

The careers of the Whallen brothers and Ben Johnson are but two examples of the political bosses existing in Kentucky who ran their machines with an iron fist and demanded loyalty and votes. The likes of Rhea, Beauchamp, Galvin, Broadbent and Klair, and especially Whallen and Johnson, are not likely to be seen again. They are an interesting piece of American history and a reflection of the times. In some ways, they ran very efficient governments. Services were delivered fairly effectively—albeit for the purpose of generating support.

There are two types of political bosses. One holds an official position, often elected; the other operates behind the scenes as a private citizen. The Whallens were not officeholders, but Johnson was. However, all machines had the same things in common—a political boss, reliance on patronage and the spoils system and behind-the-scenes control.

6

BOPTROT

FBI Exposes Extensive Corruption

Kentucky's current constitution was adopted in 1891. For more than eighty years after its adoption, the governor dominated state government, with a weak and part-time general assembly playing a minor role in Kentucky's policy and budget matters. Lobbyists, the businesses and associations that employed them and anybody else with a special interest in state decision-making went to the governor's office for help. Regardless of political affiliation, the governor directed legislative action, and for the most part, legislators obeyed.

Starting in the 1970s, general assembly members sought independence from the executive branch and an equal role in governing the commonwealth. Although they could only legislate during a brief sixty-day session every other year, the lawmakers developed an interim committee system to review issues year-round and a larger and stronger legislative staff to help the general assembly become better informed and more responsive to the public.

In 1979, Kentucky voters approved a constitutional amendment to change legislative elections to even-numbered years, separating those elections from gubernatorial elections and giving legislators more independence from the governor. In the 1980s, as the legislature grew stronger, lobbyists and their employers spent more of their time and money building relationships with legislators, often by wining and dining them in Frankfort and paying for out-of-state trips during which lobbyists had up-close access to lawmakers, developing connections that could lead to future legislative support.

In the United States, there are only a handful of state legislatures that are even close to "full time." The vast majority of states, including Kentucky, require legislators to leave home for a few months each year to meet in session and a few days each month between sessions. Although Kentucky legislators receive a salary and expenses for their time in Frankfort, it is likely that many of them have historically believed they are underappreciated and undercompensated for time spent away from their families and their regular jobs. That attitude may have been particularly prevalent in the 1980s and 1990s as legislators were called on to spend more time at the capitol than their predecessors. If lobbyists wanted to help by buying them meals or treating them to a few days in Florida, many legislators saw that as a well-deserved perk that was part of their public service.

During this period, there were no clear rules on lobbying and legislative ethics, and some legislators gladly accepted lobbyists' hospitality, including trips, meals and even cash. This was the culture that resulted in Operation BOPTROT, the FBI's undercover investigation of Kentucky legislators and lobbyists. By the time it was over, seventeen current and former legislators had been convicted, along with two top lobbyists, the Jockeys' Guild Inc., the owner of a southern Kentucky racetrack and a governor's nephew who worked in his uncle's administration.

By uncovering and prosecuting various examples of legislative corruption, the FBI and Kentucky's U.S. attorneys demonstrated that the rise of the general assembly as a coequal branch of state government was accompanied by a rise of unethical and occasionally illegal activity that influenced some of the major public policies of the 1980s and early 1990s.

BOPTROT and its related investigations touched several heavily lobbied issues, including banking and healthcare. But the scandal came to light because of a dispute between two horseracing tracks in the western Kentucky city of Henderson, located on the Ohio River, not far from Evansville, Indiana.

In March 1988, after spending over $4 million, a group of investors led by M.L. Vaughan, a Florida insurance executive and racehorse owner, reopened Henderson's old Audubon Raceway as the newly named Riverside Downs, featuring quarter-horse and harness racing. Historically, the track had a small but loyal following and coexisted with nearby Ellis Park, Henderson's Thoroughbred racetrack, because they didn't compete for bettors at the same time. That ended when Ellis joined Kentucky's three other Thoroughbred tracks by simulcasting races on their circuit and offering year-round intertrack wagering, a recent innovation that helped the tracks rake in considerably more income than live racing meets held for just a few weeks each year.[1]

Within weeks of Riverside's opening, the 1988 general assembly changed Kentucky law to grant exclusive authority to Ellis Park to conduct intertrack wagering on races from other Thoroughbred tracks, even while Riverside was featuring live racing at its track. When the new law was fully implemented, Riverside's attendance fell off dramatically as large intertrack betting pools attracted bettors to Ellis Park for televised races and intertrack wagering. "We saw our handle drop from $116,000 a night to $42,000 a night just like that," Vaughan said.[2]

Without a large metropolitan population from which to draw patrons, the competition with Ellis Park threatened Riverside's survival, so Vaughan and Riverside went to court in late 1988 to challenge the new simulcasting law. The case took more than two years to wind its way through Kentucky courts, and in the meantime, Riverside's plea for help was ignored by the 1990 general assembly.[3]

Soon after the end of the 1990 legislative session, Kentucky state senators Helen Garrett of Paducah and John Hall of Henderson both lost their bids for reelection in the May primary election and were looking at uncertain futures. Neither would be returning to Frankfort as members of the general assembly in January 1991, and their election defeats, along with their interest in staying involved in the legislative arena, may have led Garrett and Hall to engage in the corruption that launched Operation BOPTROT.

In September 1990, with Riverside on the financial ropes, Vaughan talked with Garrett, who was seeking lobbying opportunities before her term ended. Vaughan said Garrett suggested that Riverside's problems with the general assembly could be fixed, but it would cost him. "[Senator Garrett] told me she could take care of all our problems for 100 grand [$100,000]," Vaughan said in a 1992 interview.[4] "She went over how there was $10,000… for a party in Florida which that group [of legislators] is used to, you know," Vaughan recalled. "She said $30,000 in the House, $40,000 in the Senate.… And I never questioned where the other $20,000 was going to go." Vaughan said Garrett didn't go into detail, but he assumed that most of the money was to be used for payoffs.[5] Given the problems he'd had with Kentucky politicians, Vaughan was suspicious that Garrett might be setting him up.

"When all that first happened, I was afraid. It was all so blatant. It didn't set well…so [we] called the FBI," Vaughan said.[6]

Responding immediately, the FBI instructed Vaughan to call Garrett back and offer her $2,000, which she accepted. The FBI provided the money, and

Senator Helen Garrett of Paducah talks with Senator Frank Miller of Bowling Green. *Legislative Research Commission.*

Vaughan wrote Garrett a check and mailed it to her from Florida. Operation BOPTROT was underway. (In September 1992, Garrett pled guilty to mail fraud in connection with the $2,000 payment.)[7]

As they initiated their investigation, the FBI and prosecutors focused on the Business Organizations and Professions Committees (the BOP in BOPTROT) in the Kentucky State Senate and the House of Representatives. Legislators on those committees wrote (or killed) all legislation relating to Thoroughbred and harness racing (the TROT in BOPTROT).

In Kentucky, racing interests traditionally spread money around to promote favorable treatment of their industry. They were generous with their political contributions and with the lobbying perks they lavished on legislators. In addition to Frankfort hospitality like lobbyist-funded meals and drinks, Kentucky tracks regularly hosted BOP Committee meetings and trips for legislators to sunny locations like Las Vegas and Florida.

In February 1988, for example, four lobbyists and seven lawmakers flew to Pompano Beach, Florida, for a few days of eating, drinking and horse racing at the Pompano Park track. While the group was in Florida, Ellis Park owner Roger Kumar provided them with limousine service. The next month, BOP Committee members and the rest of the general assembly approved the simulcasting bill that helped Ellis Park begin to squash Riverside and enhanced Ellis's financial prospects as Kumar moved toward selling the track.[8] These regular out-of-town junkets gave racing representatives valuable opportunities to develop close working relationships with legislators, who supported or killed bills regulating their industry. The trips' appearances of impropriety made them particularly interesting to federal investigators.

As the BOPTROT investigation got underway in late 1990, the FBI seized on an opportunity presented by Henderson's soon-to-be former senator John Hall, vice-chairman of the BOP Committee. At the FBI's direction, Vaughan approached Hall about Riverside's troubles, and Hall encouraged Vaughan to go on some of the out-of-state trips, including the upcoming Jockeys' Guild convention in Las Vegas, so he could get to know BOP Committee members. "You need to go out there and wine 'em and dine 'em and give 'em a couple hundred dollars apiece," Hall told Vaughan. Hall also said Vaughan needed to hire a lobbyist, and although he was still a legislator, Hall suggested he could do the job.[9]

Vaughan agreed, and a trip to the December Jockeys' Guild convention was arranged. That's when the FBI decided to bring Chris Koumas on board to deal with Hall.

As *Courier-Journal* reporters Tom Loftus and Al Cross described it, in addition to using its own people as undercover moles, the FBI used Koumas, "a tough-talking investigator who worked for Vaughan's Florida insurance company [and] was sent in to pose as a new investor in Riverside Downs." Koumas was "a burly, bearded man who looks natural in an open-collar shirt and gold jewelry, who quickly established a rapport with Hall." Koumas accompanied Hall and other BOP Committee members to Las Vegas, and for the next year, he provided valuable undercover work for the FBI.[10]

In Las Vegas, Hall talked up Riverside to his fellow legislators while the FBI built a case against him as he requested and received $4,850, paid to him by Koumas, supposedly on behalf of Riverside. Hall agreed to use part of the money to bribe other legislators on the trip, and two of them accepted $400 each. Hall later pled guilty to extorting the bribe money from Riverside, and the two legislators pled guilty to accepting the bribes. The bribes were offered to legislators with the story that Riverside needed their help, including asking them to use their influence to persuade Governor Wallace Wilkinson to address Riverside's simulcasting issues by putting the matter on the agenda for a special legislative session, which was scheduled for the following month.

On December 21, 1990, a dozen legislators signed a letter asking Wilkinson to add the Ellis-Riverside dispute to the special session agenda. In January, just before the session convened and as Hall was leaving office, he persuaded sixty other legislators to sign a letter to Wilkinson, urging him to give the general assembly the chance to correct the discriminatory treatment of Riverside Downs. This was all to no avail. After a twenty-nine-day session, the general assembly adjourned and again Riverside was ignored. This time, Vaughan publicly blamed House Speaker Don Blandford for not persuading the governor to add the simulcast dispute to the agenda. Vaughan argued that the general assembly's poor treatment of Riverside gave Kumar (Ellis Park owner and legislative limousine provider) a stronger position as he was selling his racetrack.[11] Evidence later showed that Blandford's "hatred" of Riverside was likely a part of the track's problems with the general assembly.[12]

In February 1991, with former senator Hall now out of office and lobbying for Riverside, the FBI moved to bring him inside the tent so they could use his connections with his old colleagues. Koumas told Hall to come to Louisville, where Hall thought he was going to meet potential Riverside Downs investors. Instead, when Koumas led him into an office, he was met by FBI agents and U.S. attorneys. As Hall looked around the room, he saw large surveillance photos of himself and filing cabinets with his name on the drawers. The agents showed him videotapes and asked him about the Riverside payoff and bribes he paid in Las Vegas. Confronted with evidence that he had pocketed and paid out bribes, Hall decided to cooperate and work undercover with the investigation.[13]

Federal prosecutors and FBI agents spent the next few months determining which legislators and lobbyists were likely to have engaged in wrongdoing, who might do it again and who might lead them to other targets. Like Garrett and Hall, State Representative Bill McBee of Burlington lost in the 1990 election and returned in 1991 as a racetrack lobbyist. While in office, McBee was the longtime chairman of the House BOP Committee, and even as a former member, he still had considerable influence on the committee, particularly on racing issues.

With the FBI recognizing McBee's ongoing legislative relationships, Koumas worked to gain the trust of the newly minted lobbyist. Although the FBI didn't know it yet, McBee's legislative career included prior instances of corruption relating to racing legislation going back several years. He later pled guilty to extorting money from Dueling Grounds Race Course in Simpson County and from the Jockeys' Guild Inc. in exchange for using his

House Speaker Don Blandford confers with Representative Clay Crupper. *Legislative Research Commission.*

Representative Bill McBee became a lobbyist for Riverside Downs. *Legislative Research Commission.*

influence to pass legislation favorable to those organizations. In 1991, the FBI targeted McBee because of his legislative and racing connections and his friendship with John "Jay" Spurrier.

Spurrier was the "dean of Frankfort lobbyists" and a past chairman and current member of the Kentucky Harness Racing Commission. Koumas began passing FBI bribe money to McBee, who gave about $8,000 of it to Spurrier to get Riverside favorable racing dates from the Harness Racing Commission.[14] As the relationships developed, the FBI directed Riverside to hire Spurrier as a lobbyist, and McBee was also formally employed to promote the track's interests in the Kentucky General Assembly. An important part of Spurrier and McBee's work for Riverside was their effort to kill any attempt to enact "breed-to-breed" legislation. Under such legislation, only Thoroughbred tracks could simulcast Thoroughbred races, and harness tracks could only simulcast harness races. Thoroughbred racing is much more popular, so if breed-to-breed passed and Riverside couldn't simulcast Thoroughbreds, the track would slide further toward bankruptcy.[15]

In late 1991, Riverside and Ellis Park were scheduled to participate in a state-sponsored arbitration to determine how simulcasting dates would be divided between the tracks the following year. At an early November meeting in which Koumas was wearing a recording device, Spurrier told Koumas and McBee that he would be attending the Breeders' Cup the next day at Churchill Downs and would be sitting with the person who would appoint the state's arbitrator. Spurrier said if Riverside gave him $50,000 to spread around, he could influence the governor's choice of arbitrators and guarantee a favorable decision for the harness track. Koumas agreed.

After that, Spurrier promised $20,000 to his Breeders' Cup seatmate, the governor's nephew Bruce Wilkinson, who was in charge of appointments, including arbitrators, in his uncle's administration. Ironically, even though he committed to it, it is not clear that Wilkinson ever lifted a finger to influence the arbitration. After learning the governor planned to appoint an arbitrator, Wilkinson claimed to Spurrier that he had secured the appointment, ensuring a winning outcome for Riverside Downs. Spurrier told McBee about the deal and agreed to pay Wilkinson after the arbitrator ruled.[16]

When the arbitrator issued a favorable decision for Riverside, Spurrier and McBee cooked up a plan to collect Riverside's $50,000 and divide it among themselves and Wilkinson. They needed somebody to get the cash from Koumas so they could insulate themselves from the direct payoff. In an

Bruce Wilkinson, nephew of Governor Wallace Wilkinson and an official in his uncle's administration. *Courtesy of Kenton County Library.*

amazing stroke of luck for the FBI, Spurrier and McBee chose John Hall to handle the money, because they knew he worked for Riverside.

The plan called for Hall to get the cash from Koumas and clean up the crime by disclosing the $50,000 to the IRS as compensation for his Riverside lobbying. For handling the money, Hall could keep $20,000 to cover his tax obligation. Spurrier, McBee and Wilkinson would divide the rest. January 7, 1992, was the payoff date, and it was the day the BOPTROT investigation hit its full stride. More than forty FBI agents and U.S. attorneys converged

in June 1985. Wilkinson was elected governor of Kentucky in November 1987, and while he held that office, the conspirators did not attempt to collect any money from him.

In January 1992, when Spurrier was arrested, he told the FBI about the Banking Bill conspiracy. Spurrier agreed to cooperate with the FBI by recording conversations with the other conspirators in which they discussed their deal and their plan for obtaining their share of the bank profits from Wilkinson.

During the 1992 general assembly, in a meeting Spurrier recorded in the capitol, Rogers, Miller, Wester and Spurrier decided to get a photo of themselves standing with a life-sized cardboard photo of Wilkinson. Rogers mailed the photo to Wilkinson with a note to remind him of their deal, stating that the group "had a meeting and it was good [and] this picture just reminded me that we need to have a board of directors meeting sometime soon [and that Rogers would] be in touch."[21]

After that, Rogers and Spurrier repeatedly attempted to contact Wilkinson and met with the others to discuss the passage of the Banking Bill, the sale of the bank and their anticipated monetary gain. In an early March meeting that Spurrier recorded, Rogers referred to the potential payoff by saying, "By God…I need a little grubstake."[22]

After several unsuccessful attempts to reach the former governor to determine if the photograph Rogers sent to him had the desired effect, Spurrier enlisted the aid of Bruce Wilkinson, who later told Spurrier that his uncle refused to meet with Spurrier and the others.[23] Less than a week later, the FBI decided its nineteen months of undercover work had to end. They unsuccessfully tried to flip Bill McBee, who initially agreed to cooperate but then decided he wasn't going to blow the whistle unless he was guaranteed immunity. That night, he leaked news of the investigation to people at an end-of-session celebration at Flynn's, honoring him as Kentucky's "Lobbyist of the Year."

The next day, March 31, 1992, with its investigation compromised, the U.S. attorneys sent dozens of FBI agents to the State Capitol Building on the next-to-last day of the legislative session. Legislators, staff and the public were shocked as agents interviewed legislators, showed them videotapes of money changing hands and blanketed legislative offices with subpoenas for travel and campaign finance records.[24]

Rogers was among the many legislators interviewed at the capitol; he denied participating in any aspect of a conspiracy or attempt to extort money from Wallace Wilkinson. Rogers denied that Wilkinson owed him

From left to right: Lobbyist William Wester, Senator John Rogers, cardboard image of Governor Wallace Wilkinson, former senator Frank Miller and lobbyist Jay Spurrier. *Legislative Research Commission.*

anything, that he had any agreement with Wilkinson for his support of the Banking Bill or that he had discussed with others the amount of money owed to him by Wilkinson. After a trial in late 1994, Rogers was convicted of charges, including trying to extort money from Wilkinson and lying to the FBI, and was sentenced to forty-two months in prison.

For more than two years after the FBI raided the capitol, indictments, trials and convictions continued to play out in federal courtrooms. A last major thread of the scandal resulted in the conviction of George Atkins, a lobbyist for Humana Inc., the Kentucky-based healthcare company. Five legislators were also convicted of charges relating to their acceptance of cash from Humana lobbyists during the 1990 general assembly, when Humana was vigorously lobbying for a bill to give the corporation freedom from state control when expanding its Jefferson County hospitals.

In the end, the government succeeded in shining a light in dark corners of Kentucky's legislative process and gained convictions of public officials and private individuals and organizations for crimes relating to bills on horse racing, banking and healthcare. BOPTROT was a shock to the public system, but it focused attention on the need for reforms that would bring a greater measure of ethics and accountability to the people's house in Frankfort.

7
THE TRADITION CONTINUES

Written in 1902, this classic James Mulligan poem, "In Kentucky," captures the state's politics well. One stanza describes accurately the politics of the state's first century. Little did Mulligan know that it would stand as an apt description of Kentucky's political story from the time of its publication to the present day.

The song birds are the sweetest
In Kentucky
The thoroughbreds are the fleetest
In Kentucky
Mountains tower proudest
Thunder peals the loudest
The landscape is the grandest—
And politics—the damnedest
In Kentucky.

After many scandals and controversies throughout the history of Kentucky politics and government—has anything changed? The answer is probably yes, but not completely. While we will later discuss efforts at reform, the late twentieth and early twenty-first centuries have seen their share of political corruption. Despite much more public scrutiny, transparency and checks and balances, the tradition has continued.

There are many names associated with modern political scandals in Kentucky, and their mention immediately brings up memories of Kentucky politics at its damnedest. Some involve federal officials like Congressman Chris Perkins, who in 1994, according to Wikipedia, agreed to "plead guilty on three felony charges in connection with the U.S. House banking scandal. The following year, he was sentenced to 21 months in federal prison for misusing hundreds of thousands of dollars in campaign contributions and improperly obtaining bank loans. He was also placed on three years' supervised probation, ordered to perform 250 hours of community service, and told to complete any treatment for alcoholism deemed necessary by his probation officer."

Congressman Carroll Hubbard lost his 1992 reelection bid in the Democratic primary to Thomas Barlow. Like Perkins, Hubbard was caught up in the House banking scandal, or "Rubbergate," and he later "pleaded guilty to violations of federal campaign finance laws, and served two years in prison from 1995 to 1997. His wife, Carol Brown Hubbard, was convicted of using her husband's congressional aides to work on her campaign for Congress. She was sentenced to five years' probation."[1]

In addition to Washington, D.C. problems, Kentucky has seen several scandals at the state level in recent years. In and around state government, people in both political parties have played a role in keeping alive this aspect of a Kentucky tradition.

Richie Farmer

One of the most famous and disappointing scandals involved former high school and college basketball star Richie Farmer. He was a point guard who led Clay County High School to the Boys State Basketball Championship in 1987 and went on to enjoy a standout career at the University of Kentucky. Using his early success as a springboard, Farmer entered politics and was elected to two terms as Kentucky's commissioner of agriculture, serving from 2004 to 2012.

In 2011, he was selected to run for lieutenant governor on the ticket led by state senate president David Williams. They were defeated in the general election by Governor Steve Beshear. During the campaign, there were rumors that Farmer misused state funds and property in the Department of Agriculture. Following his term, investigations were launched, and Farmer was charged with a wide variety of crimes and violations. The Kentucky Executive Branch Ethics Commission charged him with forty-two ethics violations, more than any official in state history. Then the state's attorney general charged him with campaign finance violations. Finally, a federal grand jury indicted him on five charges of abuse of power. Farmer pled guilty in U.S. District Court and was sentenced to twenty-seven months in federal prison and ordered to pay $120,500 in restitution and $65,000 in fines. He was released from his incarceration on January 21, 2016.

BILL COLLINS

It is not every day that the spouse of a former governor is accused of extortion and disguising kickbacks. Bill Collins was the husband of former governor Martha Layne Collins, the first female governor in Kentucky's history. According to the Associated Press, "Collins, a small town dentist before his wife's rise in Kentucky Democratic politics, had been under investigation since she left office in December 1987. The lengthy investigation resulted in an indictment in July 1992 that charged he steered contracts to companies whose executives invested in his business partnerships."[2]

Many witnesses testified at Collins's trial, including his former business partner and his wife's first finance secretary, Lester "Mac" Thompson. Thompson was granted immunity and testified against Collins. The jury deliberated eleven hours before returning a guilty verdict. According to Wikipedia, Collins received a "sentence of five years and three months in federal prison, which was at the low end of the range prescribed by the federal sentencing guidelines." He was also fined $20,000 for a conspiracy charge that involved kickbacks disguised as political contributions. Former governor Collins was called to testify in the trial but was not charged. "The scandal tarnished her image and may have cost her an appointment in the administration of President Bill Clinton. Collins was also rumored to be considering running for the U.S. Senate, a bid which never materialized following her husband's conviction. Bill Collins was released from prison on October 10, 1997."[3]

Fletcher Hiring Scandal

In 2003, Ernie Fletcher became Kentucky's first Republican governor in more than thirty years. Fletcher's campaign was based in part on the idea of "cleaning up state government" after many years of Democratic control of the executive branch, and he defeated Ben Chandler, the grandson of former governor A.B. "Happy" Chandler. Ironically, after running successfully as the reform candidate, Fletcher's administration circumvented the state's employment laws to make political hires.

Fletcher's supporters argued that the attorney general's investigation of his hiring practices was overblown and that merit system abuses were a common practice of previous administrations. They said giving jobs to political supporters has been a part of the system for many years. As an example, a friend of one of this book's authors applied for a job at the Kentucky Horse Park in the early 1980s. During the interview, the friend was asked if she was registered as a Republican or a Democrat. When she answered Republican, she was told she was ineligible for the entry-level position.

However, the Fletcher administration took this hiring practice to a new level and did it in an obvious way. According to *A New History of Kentucky*, "Fletcher forces made mistakes involving the systematic and overt nature of the actions—with a 'hit list' and more—and they took illegal actions. Moreover, by using e-mails and text messaging, they left a clear electronic trail." Fletcher may have made a miscalculation by fighting the investigation rather than taking action to resolve the issues raised. Indictments followed, and Fletcher issued blanket pardons to nine administration officials, although the pardons covered many more people.

After issuing the pardons, Fletcher invoked his Fifth Amendment rights and refused to appear before the grand jury. According to *A New History of Kentucky*, these were "damning political moves." Fletcher would later be indicted on three misdemeanor counts for what the grand jury called "widespread" official misconduct for placing people in merit jobs for political reasons. He would be the third governor to be indicted in the history of the state. The other two were William S. Taylor and Flem Sampson. Taylor's indictment was related to the Goebel assassination and Sampson's to a textbook scandal. Fletcher eventually fired the nine officials involved in the scandal, and when he ran for reelection, he lost to Steve Beshear by a vote of 619,686 to 435,895.

Tim Longmeyer

Tim Longmeyer was a young, up-and-coming Democratic Party loyalist who was appointed secretary of the personnel cabinet in the administration of Steve Beshear. Attorney General Andy Beshear, Steve's son, hired Longmeyer to be a top deputy in his office, and Longmeyer resigned from that position days before he was charged with bribery.

As personnel secretary, he used his position to direct contracts to a public relations firm and received as much as $200,000 in kickbacks. It was alleged by prosecutors that part of the money was sent to the campaigns of Jack Conway for governor and Andy Beshear for attorney general. After evidence against Longmeyer was disclosed, Beshear donated the tainted money to a nonprofit organization. As personnel secretary, it was Longmeyer's job to oversee the $1.8 billion Kentucky Employees Health Plan.

Prosecutors alleged he "pushed Humana and Anthem to hire MC Squared, a public relations firm, to survey member support for their health plans. He took kickbacks from the company." Humana paid $2 million to MC Squared between 2011 and 2014, according to court documents. Longmeyer pled guilty, admitted accepting bribes and was sentenced in 2016 to six years in prison. The court rebuked him for eroding public confidence in government. According to the Associated Press, "A remorseful Longmeyer spoke at his sentencing hearing. He stayed seated, facing U.S. District Judge Karen Caldwell. He apologized to the Commonwealth, his family, federal authorities and state government employees, saying he failed to follow his 'moral compass.'"[4]

Judge Caldwell characterized Longmeyer's case as unique because he didn't use it to personally enrich himself but to enhance his political stature. "He risked it all and lost it all for political influence, for financial gain," Caldwell said. "He wanted a bigger and more influential seat at the table."[5]

Conclusion

So, the tradition has continued, at least to some extent. When thinking of modern scandals in Kentucky, it is fair to ask if the frequency has been reduced. In the most recent report of the U.S. Department of Justice's Public Integrity Section, the U.S. Attorney's Office for the Eastern District of Kentucky reports that in the ten years ending in 2018, there were 170 federal public corruption convictions in the Eastern District of Kentucky. In the same time period, there were 72 convictions in the Western District. The ten-year total for the Eastern District is the lowest total reported since at least 2011, although it's still in the top twenty in the nation and is much higher than the numbers posted for neighboring West Virginia.

In these days of greater transparency, it seems logical to believe that getting away with unethical or criminal behavior in government is much harder, but has significant reform and transparency changed the system? In Kentucky, particularly as a result of BOPTROT, the answer is probably yes. Looking at the reforms the state has made and their impact will help answer this question.

8

ETHICS LAWS AIM TO
STEM CORRUPTION

Corruption has always been part of the human experience. At some points, we all act in our own self-interest, but when those acts come at the expense of someone else or the public interest, there can be corruption, and often scandal. It happens all over the world, with public and private people and organizations, rich and poor, religious and secular, famous and unknown, so it makes sense to be skeptical of surveys or studies that purport to identify any particular nation, state, business or profession as "more corrupt" than any other, because corruption can happen anywhere.

All corruption undermines trust, but public corruption may have the most widespread and damaging impact. By undermining trust between citizens and their government, public corruption damages the chances for a community, state or nation to succeed.

Whether a scandal in government involves one person or dozens, it can affect the future of the governed. If citizens in a community or state lose faith in their government, real or perceived, political instability can threaten the type of economic and social development needed to keep or attract people, businesses and jobs.

As described in the preceding chapters of this book, Kentucky has a history of political corruption and public scandal. While other states have similar stories to tell, corruption has been particularly detrimental to Kentucky's economic well-being. Corruption in the state has contributed to and been exacerbated by poverty, substandard educational opportunities, poor health, isolated communities and inadequate infrastructure. In large parts of the state, foreign corporations extracted much of Kentucky's mineral wealth, shipped the profits out of state and left corrupted governments, weak economies, sick employees, damaged land and water or a combination thereof.

All those issues help explain why Kentucky and West Virginia are usually found together in or near the bottom ten states in U.S. rankings of employment, job growth, per capita GDP, GDP growth, average weekly wages and wage growth.[1]

So, when public corruption comes to light through the efforts of law enforcement or journalists, it is vitally important that affected governments start immediately to rebuild the trust of the citizenry and try to avoid long-term social and economic damage. In the 1990s, after scandals on the state and local levels, the Kentucky General Assembly did just that by taking several important steps toward establishing ethics laws to guide state legislators, executive branch officials and employees and local government officials.

CODE OF LEGISLATIVE ETHICS

Perhaps because of the scope and seriousness of the BOPTROT scandal, the legislative ethics code adopted in 1993 is the strongest and most comprehensive of the three ethics laws. Many of the code's provisions were in direct response to criminal acts in BOPTROT. For example, several of the people convicted were former legislators who moved directly into lobbying when they left the Kentucky General Assembly. Therefore, the code includes a two-year "cooling off" period before a former legislator can register to lobby—among the strictest revolving-door provisions in the nation.

Also, when several BOPTROT legislators were convicted after unsuccessfully arguing that payments received from lobbyists were campaign contributions, a statute was adopted prohibiting legislators and legislative candidates from taking campaign contributions from lobbyists—again, one of the strictest prohibitions of its kind in the United States.

As described in chapter six, the pre-BOPTROT years were a time of unlimited wining, dining and travel for legislators, paid for by lobbyists and businesses and organizations that employed lobbyists. That unregulated atmosphere led directly to the improper relationships that were at the root of BOPTROT. The 1993 general assembly, led by newly elected Speaker Joe

In any event, Kentucky taxpayers and the Legislative Ethics Commission paid over $50,000 for Attorney General Andy Beshear's office to defend the ethics law against Schickel's attack. During the case, several lobbying organizations joined as friends of the court to support the constitutionality of the lobbying restrictions. The Kentucky Chamber of Commerce, Kentucky League of Cities, Kentucky Coal Association and Kentucky Nonprofit Network argued that the ethics law successfully combats corruption and that invalidating the law could bring chaos in lobbying activities.[3]

On May 30, 2019, the U.S. Court of Appeals for the Sixth Circuit upheld all provisions of Kentucky's legislative ethics law that were challenged by Schickel, sending a clear signal for strong public ethics laws across the nation. Schickel lost his case in a unanimous decision by a panel of judges appointed by Presidents George W. Bush, Jimmy Carter and Donald Trump. In late 2019, the U.S. Supreme Court denied Schickel's request that the nation's highest court review the case.

Kentucky's legislative ethics law is strengthened by the decisive ruling of the U.S. Court of Appeals that the law is consistent with the U.S. Constitution. The federal court ruling in the Schickel case is an important message to the other forty-nine states, hundreds of cities and counties and to the U.S. Congress that they can adopt strong ethics laws like Kentucky's and help public officials and lobbyists avoid corruption.

For twenty-seven years, the ethics law has helped Kentucky prevent the legislative corruption that has plagued most other states. In those years, no Kentucky legislator has been indicted or convicted for misusing his or her public office, while dozens of legislators in other states have gone to prison.

The law has served Kentucky well by helping citizens and legislators work in a more ethical culture, so the general assembly can build and maintain the confidence of the public.

Executive Branch Code of Ethics

In 1991, when Brereton Jones campaigned in the Kentucky gubernatorial election, he promised he would bring ethics reform to the governor's office and the executive branch of state government. Several prior administrations had experienced controversies, including allegations and stories of real and perceived corruption. As a horse farm owner who had

Governor Brereton Jones. *Kenton County Library.*

only spent four years in Kentucky state government as lieutenant governor, Jones tried to take the high road on ethics and frequently said he wanted to take the "For Sale" sign off the capitol.[4]

Jones won the 1991 election by a record margin of 246,000 votes, and one minute after he was sworn in at 12:01 a.m. on December 10, he signed Kentucky's first code of ethics for the executive branch of state government.

Among other provisions, Jones's original code prohibited state employees from disclosing confidential information acquired in the course of their duties to further their own or others' economic interests, holding a state lease or contract, soliciting gifts from people who want to do business with the state or accepting any gift valued at more than $200 from any people seeking to do business with the state. It also prohibited former state employees from taking a job within six months of leaving state government with a company they regulated when they were in government. The code

> *local government elective offices, elected officials of each city, county or consolidated local government, and other officials or employees of the city, county, or consolidated local government, as specified in the code of ethics;*
> *(c) A policy on the employment of members of the families of officials or employees of the city, county or consolidated local government, as specified in the code of ethics; and*
> *(d) The designation of a person or group who shall be responsible for enforcement of the code of ethics, including maintenance of financial disclosure statements, all of which shall be available to the public.*

Although the legislation did not specify how each of those areas would be addressed, Callahan said that in cities and counties where the public got involved in the process, the ethics codes would reflect that interest and would be effective in guiding the local officials toward ethical behavior. Cities and counties had until January 1, 1995, to enact a code by local ordinance. Those failing to do so became ineligible to receive state funds.

It appears that Callahan was correct in predicting that the outcomes would vary based on the level of interest shown by the local citizenry. In early 1995, historian and author Thomas Parrish and veteran Kentucky journalist Al Smith wrote an article about the new law for the Shakertown Roundtable:

> *As might be expected, the* [ethics] *codes process produced varying results across the state. Callahan declared himself "ecstatic" over developments in Northern Kentucky—his home area, specifically, the involvement of citizens of Kenton County, where a 16-person commission drew up the ethics code. In other areas as well, he said, "people are stepping forward to advocate strong ethics laws." In Bardstown and Nelson County, for instance, a six-person board formulated the local code. The point here, said Callahan, is that "the ethical behavior of local officials has become an issue in a way that would not have been possible if the General Assembly had simply dictated a set of rules for officeholders to follow."*

Elsewhere, as Callahan conceded, the picture has clearly been less satisfactory, as fiscal courts and city councils have taken little initiative to involve the public, and the public has not on its own demanded strong guidelines. "That is not the fault of the legislation," Callahan declared. "It is the fault of the electorate." Some governing bodies have obviously felt that ethical standards are nobody's business but their own. While going through the motions of drafting ethics legislation, as an observer noted, one county judge won high marks for candor if not conscientiousness by openly declaring that if he couldn't hire his relatives, then they wouldn't have any reason to vote for him. But if city commissions and fiscal courts do not prove responsive to the public will, Callahan declared, "the public can always declare its disapproval at the next election."[8]

In October 1997, almost three years after the local codes took effect, the Associated Press reported on the mixed results:

> *Most cities and counties required political candidates to report sources of income over $5,000 or $10,000. Some ethics boards have never met. Each county and city keep its own records. Relatively few appear to have had anything to record: In Franklin County, a magistrate serving on the Kentucky Association of Counties was fined $300 for a conflict of interest. He had voted to have the county instead of the association pay claims against an ousted jailer. The ethics board in Paducah recently fined three of four commissioners $200 each for giving themselves raises above the increase in the cost of living. A Magoffin County ethics board forced some county workers to pay delinquent garbage bills. In Fayette County, four complaints filed by a watchdog group called Citizens for Ethical Government have yet to produce any significant results, said Paul O'Brian, a group founder.*
>
> *"This gave them a shell and let them build inside that shell," said Representative James Callahan (D-Southgate), who sponsored the legislation. "I really think it's working very well."[9]*

CONCLUSION

Like most states, Kentucky has a long and interesting past of significant accomplishments colored by a hidden history of political scandals. The commonwealth has come a long way since the early days of statehood, and our past has helped shape aggressive efforts at reform in hopes of stemming both the severity and prevalence of corruption.

By several objective measures, these efforts have been quite successful. However, human nature being what it is, corruption and scandals will always be with us. We credit the generations of whistleblowers, law enforcement, journalists and citizens who have exposed and described instances of corrupt behavior. It is important to recognize that most public servants, elected and appointed, are honorably serving their community, state and nation every day.

In those instances where dishonesty or corruption seeks an opportunity, we all play a role in preventing corruption in our public affairs. According to G. Edward Griffin, "To oppose corruption in government is the highest obligation of patriotism."

Notes

Introduction

1. Fredrick J. Turner, "The Origin of Genet's Projected Attack on Louisiana and the Floridas," *American Historical Review* 3, no. 4 (July 1898): 652.
2. Pearce, *Divide and Dissent*, 1.

Chapter One

1. Watlington, *The Partisan Spirit*, 3.
2. Ibid., 17.
3. Ibid., 40.
4. Ibid., 43.
5. Clinger and Hall, *Kentucky Government, Politics, and Public Policy*, 10.
6. Ibid, 10.
7. Frank Mathias, "The Turbulent Years of Kentucky Politics, 1820–1850," *Register of Kentucky Historical Society* (Summer 1990): 311.
8. Ibid., 312.
9. Ibid.
10. Ibid., 313.
11. Wikipedia, "Jonathan Cilley."
12. Ibid.

Chapter Two

1. Glen Taul and Dennis Fielding, "Politics and Corruption in Antebellum Kentucky," *Register of the Kentucky Historical Society* 89, no. 3 (Summer 1991): 241.
2. Ibid., 243–44.
3. Ibid., 256.
4. Ibid., 261.
5. Louis DeFalaise, "General Stephen Gano Burbridge's Command in Kentucky," *Register of the Kentucky Historical Society* 69, issue 2 (April 1971): 101–27.
6. Proclamation 113, by Abraham Lincoln, Declaring Martial Law and a Further Suspension of the Writ of Habeas Corpus in Kentucky (1864), en.wikisource.org/wiki/Proclamation_113.
7. *Owensboro (KY) Monitor*, November 16, 1864, 3.
8. DeFalaise, "General Stephen Gano Burbridge's Command," 101–27.
9. Klotter and Friend, *A New History of Kentucky*, 223.
10. Ibid., 224.
11. Ibid., 226.
12. Tapp and Klotter, *Kentucky Decades of Discord 1865–1900*, 5.
13. Klotter and Friend, *A New History of Kentucky*, 239.
14. Tapp and Klotter, *Kentucky: Decades of Discord*, 8.
15. Ibid., 9.
16. Harrison, *Kentucky Governors: 1792–1985*, 81.
17. Ibid., 80–81.
18. Marion Lucas, "Kentucky Blacks Transition from Slavery to Freedom," *Register of the Kentucky Historical Society*, 412.
19. Wikipedia, "Preston Leslie."
20. Historyengine.richmond.edu.
21. Craig, *True Tales of Old-Time Kentucky Politics*, 90.
22. Klotter, *Breckinridges of Kentucky*, v.
23. Miller, *Bringing Down the Colonel*, 14.
24. Ibid., 183.

Chapter Three

1. *Courier-Journal*, March 21, 1888, 1.
2. Perrin, Kniffin and Battle, *Kentucky: A History of the State*.
3. Klotter and Friend, *A New History of Kentucky*, 163–64.

4. John McAfee, *Kentucky Politicians. Sketches of representative Corncrackers and other miscellany.*

5. *Louisville Daily Journal,* September 27, 1867, 1.

6. Tapp and Klotter, *Kentucky: Decades of Discord,* 244.

7. *Courier-Journal,* March 29, 1888, 3.

8. *Stanford (Kentucky) Interior Journal,* February 14, 1888, 2.

9. *Owensboro Messenger,* February 7, 1885, 2.

10. *Hazel Green Herald,* June 24, 1885, 2.

11. *Owensboro Messenger,* July 11, 1885, 1.

12. Ibid., July 9, 1885, 1.

13. *(Hartford) Ohio County News,* August 19, 1885, 2.

14. *Courier-Journal,* May 5, 1887, 1.

15. *(Maysville) Evening Bulletin,* September 10, 1887, 3; *Frankfort Roundabout,* September 10, 1887, 5.

16. Tapp and Klotter, *Kentucky: Decades of Discord,* 231.

17. Ibid., 235.

18. *Owensboro Messenger,* November 12, 1887, 2.

19. Tapp and Klotter, *Kentucky: Decades of Discord,* 242.

20. *Courier-Journal,* March 22, 1888, 1.

21. McQueen, *Offbeat Kentuckians: Legends to Lunatics,* 75.

22. *Courier-Journal,* March 21, 1888, 1; March 22, 1888, 1.

23. Ibid., March 21, 1888, 1.

24. Ibid.

25. Ibid.

26. Ibid.

27. *Owensboro Messenger & Examiner,* April 12, 1888, 1.

28. Tapp and Klotter, *Kentucky: Decades of Discord,* 242.

29. *Owensboro Messenger & Examiner,* April 5, 1888, 2.

30. *Courier-Journal,* August 9, 1890, 3.

31. *(Maysville) Public Ledger,* December 21, 1895, 2.

32. *Courier-Journal,* August 7, 1906, 3.

33. *(Birmingham, Alabama) Evening News,* August 7, 1889, 1.

34. *(Vicksburg, Mississippi) Daily Commercial Herald,* September 28, 1890, 5.

35. *Chicago Tribune,* September 26, 1897, 33.

36. *Courier-Journal,* July 20, 1897, 5.

37. *Salt Lake Telegram,* July 29, 1902, 2.

38. *New York Times,* January 22, 1898, 1.

Chapter Four

1. Klotter and Friend, *A New History of Kentucky*, 226.
2. Garry Adelman, American Battlefield Trust, and Woodside, Mary Bays, "A House Divided: Civil War Kentucky," *Hallowed Ground Magazine*, April 16, 2010.
3. Christopher Phillips, "How Kentucky Became a Confederate State," *New York Times*, May 22, 2015.
4. Marianne C. Walker, "The Late Governor Goebel: He Fought, Killed, and Was Killed," *Humanities* 34, no. 4 (July/August 2013).
5. Klotter, *William Goebel: The Politics of Wrath*, 21.
6. Walker, *Humanities*.
7. *San Francisco Call* 77, no. 123, April 12, 1895.
8. Walker, *Humanities*.
9. Klotter, *William Goebel: The Politics of Wrath*, 65.
10. Ibid., 67.
11. Ibid., 79.
12. Ibid., 72.
13. *Courier-Journal*, September 2, 1899, 1.
14. "Milton H. Smith Talks About the Goebel Affair," *Register of the Kentucky Historical Society* 78, no. 4 (Autumn 1980), edited by Edison H. Thomas, note on page 333.
15. *Courier-Journal (Louisville)*, October 19, 1899, 1.
16. Klotter, *William Goebel: The Politics of Wrath*, 82.
17. *Courier-Journal*, November 7, 1899, 1.
18. Edward Foley, "Ballot Battles: The History of Disputed Elections in the United States," 170–71.
19. Pearce, *Days of Darkness*, 188.
20. Ibid., 188–89.
21. *Courier-Journal*, January 16, 1900, 1.
22. Ibid., January 17, 1900, 1.
23. Ibid., January 24, 1900, 6.
24. Thomas D. Clark, "The People, William Goebel, and the Kentucky Railroads," *Journal of Southern History* 5, no. 1 (February 1939): 45–46.
25. *Courier-Journal*, January 30, 1900, 1.
26. Ibid., January 31, 1900, 1.
27. Ibid.
28. *Courier-Journal*, February 1, 1900.
29. *Taylor and Marshall v. Beckham*, 178 U.S. 548 (1900).

Chapter Five

1. Klotter and Friend, *A New History of Kentucky*, 263.
2. Tracy Campbell, "How to Steal an Election," *Kentucky Humanities*, April 2006, 3.
3. Wikipedia, "Secret Ballots."
4. Campbell, "How to Steal an Election," 4.
5. Kleber, *Kentucky Encyclopedia*, 946.
6. Duane Bolin, *Kentucky Gazette*, August 2019, 5.
7. Campbell, *Kentucky Humanities*, 8.
8. Ibid.
9. Ibid., 10.
10. Campbell, *Deliver the Vote*, 130.
11. Kleber, *Kentucky Encyclopedia*, 472.
12. Ibid.
13. James Klotter and John Muir, "Boss Ben Johnson, the Highway Commission, and Kentucky Politics, 1927–1937," *Register of the Kentucky Historical Society* 84, no. 1 (Winter 1986): 23–24.
14. Ibid., 22.
15. Ibid., 25.
16. Ibid., 30.
17. Ibid., 33.
18. See Arthur H. Estabrook, "Poor Relief in Kentucky," *Social Science Review* 3 (1929): 224–42 (as identified by Klotter and Muir).

Chapter Six

1. Bob Lewis, "Henderson Racetrack Owner Says His Dream Turned Into Nightmare," *Paducah Sun*, November 8, 1992, 9A.
2. Ibid.
3. *Tri-City Turf v. Public Protection and Regulation Cabinet*, 806 S.W.2d 394 (Ky. App., 1991).
4. Lewis, *Paducah Sun*, 9A.
5. Tom Loftus, "Anatomy of a Scandal," *Courier-Journal*, July 30, 1995, 33.
6. Lewis, *Paducah Sun*, 9A.
7. Tom Loftus and Al Cross, "Lies, Bribes & Videotapes," *State Legislatures*, July 1993, 42.

BIBLIOGRAPHY

Bolin, James Duane. *Bossism and Reform in a Southern City: Lexington, Kentucky 1880–1940*. Lexington: University of Kentucky Press, 2000.

Campbell, Tracy. *Deliver the Vote*. New York: Carroll & Graf, 2005.

———. *The Politics of Despair: Power and Resistance in the Tobacco Wars*. Lexington: University Press of Kentucky, 1993.

Clinger, James C., and Michael W. Hail. *Kentucky Government, Politics and Public Policy*. Lexington: University Press of Kentucky, 2013.

Craig, Berry. *True Tales of Old-Time Kentucky Politics: Bombast, Bourbon & Burgoo*. Charleston, SC: The History Press, 2009.

Foley, Edward. *Ballot Battles: The History of Disputed Elections in the United States*. New York: Oxford University Press, 2016.

Harrison, Lowell. *Kentucky Governors: 1792–1985*. Lexington: University Press of Kentucky, 1985.

Harrison, Lowell H., and James C. Klotter. *A New History of Kentucky*. Lexington: University Press of Kentucky, 1997.

Kleber, John, ed. *The Kentucky Encyclopedia*. Lexington: University Press of Kentucky, 1992.

Klotter, James. *The Breckinridges of Kentucky 1760–1981*. Lexington: University Press of Kentucky, 1986.

———. *William Goebel: The Politics of Wrath*. Lexington: University Press of Kentucky, 1977.

Klotter, James, and Craig Thompson Friend. *A New History of Kentucky*. 2nd ed. Lexington: University Press of Kentucky, 2018.

McAfee, John. *Kentucky Politicians: Sketches of representative Corncrackers and other miscellany*. Louisville, KY: Press of the Courier-Journal Job Printing Company, 1886.

McQueen, Keven. *Offbeat Kentuckians: Legends to Lunatics*. Kuttawa, KY: McClanahan Publishing House, 2001.

Miller, Patricia. *Bringing Down the Colonel*. New York: Sarah Crichton Books, 2018.

Pearce, John Ed. *Days of Darkness: The Feuds of Eastern Kentucky*. Lexington: University Press of Kentucky, 1994.

———. *Divide and Dissent*. Lexington: University Press of Kentucky, 1991.

Perrin, William, G.C. Kniffin and J.H. Battle. *Kentucky: A History of the State*. 5th ed. Louisville, KY: F.A. Battey, 1887.

Tapp, Hambleton, and James C. Klotter. *Kentucky: Decades of Discord 1865–1900*. Frankfort: Kentucky Historical Society, 1977.

Watlington, Patricia. *The Partisan Spirit*. Atheneum, 1972.

Index

About the Authors

Robert Schrage is very active in local history circles and has served on the boards of the Rabbit Hash Historical Society, Boone County Historic Preservation Board and the Behringer Crawford Board. In 2015, Schrage received the William Conrad Preservation Excellence Award for Lifetime Achievement in preservation of local history. Previous works include *Lost Northern Kentucky* (The History Press), *Legendary Locals of Covington* (Arcadia), *Eyewitness to History: A Personal Journal* (winner of honorable mentions at the New York, Amsterdam and Florida Book Festivals [Merlot Group]), *Carl Kiger: The Man Beyond the Murder* (Merlot Group), *The Ohio River from Cincinnati to Louisville* (Arcadia), *Boone County: Then and Now* (Arcadia) and *Burlington* (Arcadia).

John Schaaf retired as executive director of the Kentucky Legislative Ethics Commission, where he worked for fifteen years, and served on the steering committee of the international Council on Governmental Ethics Laws. Prior to that, he was the general counsel for the Kentucky Legislative Research Commission, as well as an attorney with a Louisville law firm and a brief stint as editor of a weekly newspaper. Schaaf received a degree in journalism from the University of Kentucky and his JD from the Louis D. Brandeis School of Law at the University of Louisville. This is his first effort at writing a book.